**TREES ARE SO BIG AND TOUGH
NOTHING CAN INJURE THEM!**

Trees in cities and forests worldwide are being mutilated, and many are dying because of abuses by people and their activities.

1

**Myth 2. TREES ARE A NATURAL RENEWABLE RESOURCE.
KEEP CUTTING. THEY WILL GROW BACK JUST AS THEY WERE.**
    Yes, some trees in forests should be cut for the needs of people. But, better
management schemes are needed to ensure a continuing supply of high quality
trees and to ensure that all connected members of the natural systems continue
to survive in a high quality state.

REMEMBER,
IT IS NOT HOW MUCH YOU KNOW,
BUT HOW MUCH YOU KNOW
THAT IS CORRECT THAT MAKES YOU WISE!

Myth 3. **NATURE IS BALANCED.**

Balance means the equalization of opposing forces. Natural systems survive because they are in continuing states of dynamic equilibrium. They vibrate. They adjust to a continuing feedback process for survival. Natural systems are not balanced in the sense of no motion or no change. They are not static.

Myth 4. **FORESTS ARE GROUPS OF TREES.**

Forests are highly ordered connections of many living communities with trees. The connections ensure survival of the trees and their associates.

MYTHS: HOW DO THEY START?

MYTHS are usually started and spread by people who are well-meaning and dedicated to causes they may or may not understand. Myths often start from attempts to define reality when information is lacking.

Because myths often come from good people and organizations, the attempt to discard a myth is taken often as an insult by some people or organizations.

An example is Myth 5. Many good people and organizations are telling everybody to plant trees, implying that anybody can plant a tree correctly. Sad, but true, incorrect planting, and planting the wrong tree in the wrong place have led to serious tree problems worldwide. Yes, we should plant trees. But, first we need to know the correct way to do it and to get that information out to the people.

TREE MYTHS

MYTH is used in this book to include misconceptions, misunderstandings, and, mostly, half truths.

MANY of the corrections to the myths listed here are known by many people. Then, why do they persist? I believe they persist because many of the myths taken alone appear trivial, or a matter of semantics. The problem is that these trivial-appearing myths are often combined with those that can cause serious injuries, such as flush cuts, paints, and cavity cleaning. Each myth is like a thread. When a hundred or more weak threads are used to make a fabric called a tree care profession, the profession will be only as strong as the threads that form it. There is more. Natural systems have more variables than any other system on earth. The responsibility of tree care professionals is to manage a large part of that system in ways that will benefit all members of the system. Not an easy task! Because there are so many parts of the natural systems that are beyond our regulation, we need every bit of clarity, exactness, and sound understanding of those parts we can regulate. Then, and only then, will we be able to manage tree systems, and environmental systems, in ways that ensure high quality survival for all of the connected members.

In my book **Modern Arboriculture,** I list 409 research papers by others who have provided information on many of the subjects discussed in this book. When papers by others are cited in this book, the numbers for the papers as listed in **Modern Arboriculture** references — pages 391 to 406 — are given after the letter X. For example, X-191 is a paper by Liese, W. and Dujesiefken, D., and X-130 is a book by R.W. Harris.

I strongly encourage all readers to study also books on trees and their correct care written by *other* authors. Some books to start with are those by Drs. J. Feucht, R. Harris, R. Miller, T. Kozlowski, and P.P. Pirone. Here are some other books by other authors that I recommend, as cited in **Modern Arboriculture:** X-7, 20, 21, 22, 23, 42, 43, 60, 86, 91, 93, 106, 120, 130, 133, 134, 135, 136, 141, 180, 214, 231, 292, 336, 357, 359, 389, 396, 407, and 408.

Where each subject in this book is mentioned in my other books, the letter indicates the book, and the number indicates the page.

Reference Codes
Books by Dr. Alex L. Shigo

A. A New Tree Biology   H. Tree Pruning
B. A New Tree Biology Dictionary   M. Modern Arboriculture

For information on obtaining copies of A, B, H, and M, and for slide packages, booklets, audio cassettes, posters, video, and for bulk orders of this book and other items, contact the publisher:

Shigo and Trees, Associates
P.O. Box 769, Durham, NH 03824-0769 U.S.A.
603 868 7459   Fax: 603 868 1045

IT IS NOT HOW FAST YOU ARE MOVING, BUT YOUR DIRECTION TOWARD A TARGET THAT MAKES YOU SUCCESSFUL!

THE RUSH IS ON TO PLANT TREES.

Myth 5.   **ANYBODY CAN PLANT A TREE CORRECTLY!**
KINGS, QUEENS, PRESIDENTS, GOVERNORS, and many organizations worldwide are telling people to plant trees. The implication is that *anybody* can plant a tree correctly. (See article by Ted Williams in *Audubon*, May, 1991.)

Incorrect planting procedures, and planting the wrong tree in the wrong place have caused a multitude of tree problems worldwide. It is not only bad that money is wasted for the purchase of the tree, but it is sad when the dignity of the tree is destroyed as it wanes and dies standing tightly bound in place for all to see. This has to be one of the worst injustices humankind has inflicted on nature.

Yes, trees should be planted. They should be planted correctly. Or if correct planting procedures are not known, then trees should be planted under the supervision of a tree care professional who understands how to plant correctly, and who understands the concept of the right tree in the right place. And, after planting, a continuing health care schedule should be maintained.

On the next two pages I have illustrations and summary comments on incorrect and correct planting procedures.

Humans have caused many injuries to natural systems
because of greed and ignorance.
Injury because of ignorance will diminish as
better educational schemes are developed.
Greed will diminish as leaders show that correct management
schemes profit natural systems and business.

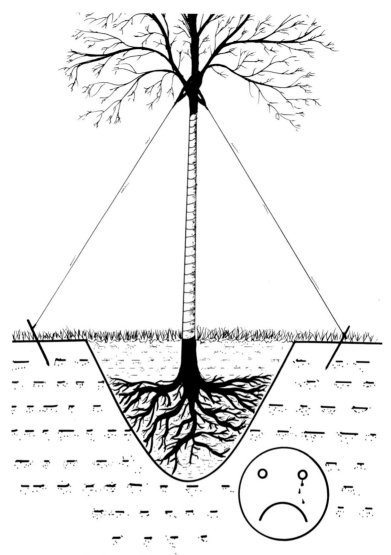

DO NOT PLANT TOO DEEP

- Money is wasted when trees are planted too deep.
- Do not bury roots in small deep holes.
- Do not wrap trees.
- Do not amend the soil, unless the soil is very poor.
- Do not brace so tightly that the tree cannot sway.
- Do not brace with wire in a hose.
- Do not fertilize at planting time.
- Do not plant grass or flowers near the tree.
- Do not remove branches to balance crown with roots.

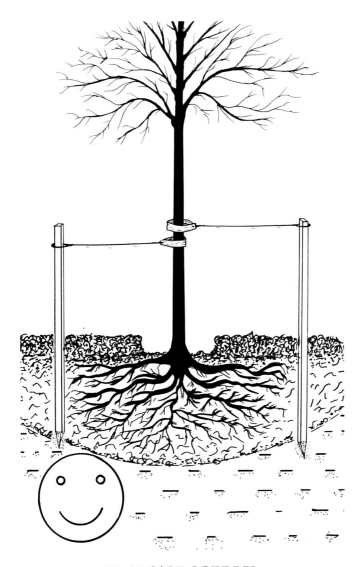

PLANT PROPERLY

- Plant at the depth where roots spread from the trunk.
- Prepare a planting site, not just a hole in the ground.
- Loosen the soil far beyond the dripline of the tree.
- Brace the tree only if it will not remain upright in a moderate wind.
- Brace with broad, belt-like materials that won't injure the bark.
- Mulch away from the trunk with composted material.
- Keep soil moist, not water-logged, to the depth of the roots.
- Remove dead and dying branches.
- Wait until the second growing season to begin training cuts for shaping and to begin fertilizing.

NEVER IN THE HISTORY OF HUMANKIND HAVE SO MANY PEOPLE TALKED SO MUCH ABOUT WHAT THEY UNDERSTAND SO LITTLE — THE ENVIRONMENT.

THE DANGEROUS HALF TRUTH.

Many of the myths given in this book are really half truths, where the wrong part has become the accepted part.

Other myths are really half truths because of dose. And, again, the extremes in dosage have become the problem. For example, water can be very beneficial or very harmful depending on dose. The same can be said for pruning, mulching, fertilizing, and amending soils.

THE DEMAND FOR BROAD RECIPES IS THE MAJOR PROBLEM.

A professional is a person who understands dose! And, an understanding of dose depends on an understanding of the system that is to be treated (M-32).

Training without education makes robots.
Education without training makes waste.
Both are needed; training and education.

MYTHS

Myth 6. PLANT DEEP AND ROOTS WILL GROW DEEPER.

If the roots survive, they will grow upward (B-94, M-310). Some tree species such as green ash, *Fraxinus pennsylvanica*, and honey locust, *Gleditsia triacanthos*, survive deep planting because they generate new roots higher on the buried trunk. Deep planting may not lead to early death on other species, but the roots growing upward often break sidewalks and cause lawn problems. Cutting the surface roots causes the tree more injury. The best solution is to mulch over the grass and woody surface roots. Using root barriers just puts the tree back in a pot. If roots do emerge from the bottom of a barrier, the roots usually grow upward, not downward deeper into the soil.

Myth 7. BEFORE PLANTING, PRUNE LIVING BRANCHES
TO BALANCE CROWN WITH ROOTS.

Removing living branches takes food from the tree. Dr. W. Merrill and Dr. E.B. Cowling showed that as living cells in wood age and die, nitrogen "moves" out to the younger living cells (X-226). Twigs, branches, and trunks of trees have billions of living cells that store energy reserves, usually as starch or oils. As leaves, twigs, and branches die, these reserves "move" back into the remaining living cells in branches and trunk. To remove the living branches before the energy reserves have had time to relocate takes energy from the tree. Wait until the branches die, then remove them correctly. Do remove dead and injured branches at planting time. (See also X-127.)

Myth 8. LOTS OF MULCH IS GOOD.

Mulch is too thick when roots start growing into it. When roots are growing in the mulch, several continuous hot dry days can lead to root death. Mulch is very beneficial for trees. Start by applying 3 to 4 inches (7 to 10 cm.) and inspect the mulch several times a year for root growth. Keep mulch at least 6 inches (15 cm.) away from the trunk to reduce chances of rodent injury and infection by pathogens. Excessive amounts of mulch may disrupt soil moisture and aeration. It is best to keep adding small amounts of composted material over time. (See X-93.)

Myth 9. LOTS OF SOIL AMENDMENTS
ARE GOOD IN THE PLANTING SITE.

Do not amend the planting site when the soil is good. When the planting site contains old building rubble, or if the soil has poor structure, or lacks essential elements, and trees must be planted in such sites, amendments are necessary. There are no simple general recipes to fit all situations. If the planting site is to be amended, then the mature size of the tree should be considered, and a large enough volume of soil should be amended to meet the requirements of the growing tree. (See X-91, 92, 93, 130, and 231.)

Myth 10.   AFTER PLANTING, BRACE THE TREE TIGHTLY.
If bracing is needed, the tree should be able to sway (X-130). There is an old farmer's term, feathering, that means movement of a plant as it grows leads to a more sturdy plant. See research by Dr. C. Matthech (X-208, 209, and 210) that describes the way trees respond to sudden loss of branches that affects movement and stabilization of the remaining trunk. Research by Dr. Anthony J. Trewavas (see Proceedings of the National Academy of Sciences, June 1992 for more) showed that movement stimulated proteins to bond with calcium, thus strengthening cell walls.

Myth 11.   USE WIRE IN A HOSE TO BRACE TREES.
Use broad, belt-like strapping that will not injure bark (H-177). Regardless of what type of support is used, the support should be removed as soon as the tree is sturdy in the soil. Too often trees are planted deeply to avoid the need for bracing. Another problem is that the tree may be already too deep in a wire basket or burlap bag, and the person planting it thinks that the depth of planting should be at the point where the bag is tied.

IF PEOPLE DEFINED THEIR TERMS, ARGUMENTS WOULD BE LESS THAN THREE MINUTES.   *Voltaire*

KNOW THE PERSON BY THE WORDS THEY USE.   *Socrates*

MYTHS START WHEN PEOPLE USE TERMS THAT THEY CANNOT DEFINE.   *Shigo*

For an excellent discussion on terms, see Kloepper J.W. *et al.,* Proposed Elimination of the Term Endorhizosphere, 1992, Phytopathology 82: 726-727. This paper discusses some of the problems that arise when poorly defined terms are used. Also, see my paper on terms in Agricultural Research, U.S. Dept. Agr., Agr. Res. Ser. 35, No 5, 1987.

Myth 12.   WOOD IS DEAD.
 In a living tree there are more living cells in sapwood than dead cells. There
are no living cells in heartwood, wetwood, discolored wood, and false heartwood. Wood is a highly ordered arrangement of living, dying, and dead cells.
The cell walls are made up of cellulose, lignin, and hemicelluloses. Vessels and
tracheids are very large compared to axial and radial parenchyma cells. Vessels,
fibers, and tracheids live only a short time. Therefore, on a volume basis,
sapwood is mostly dead, and on a number-of-cell basis, sapwood is mostly alive
(M-273, X-342).

Myth 13.   TREES HEAL WOUNDS.
 Trees cannot restore injured tissues in their same spatial position. Trees
are generating systems. Trees form new cells in new spatial positions throughout their lives. Heal means to restore in the same spatial position. Animals are
regenerating systems that form new cells, and new cell parts in their previously
occupied spatial positions. When injured, animals speed up their normal
regenerating processes, and this is called healing. When trees are injured and
infected they chemically strengthen their boundaries that resist spread of
infections in wood extant at time of wounding, — reaction zone — and then
trees form another new anatomical and chemical boundary that separates the
infected wood from the new healthy wood that continues to form — barrier
zone. This defense process in trees is called compartmentalization (see **A New
Tree Biology** and the many research papers listed in this book that support this
concept).

ENVIRONMENT IS A COLLECTION OF THINGS AROUND YOU.

NATURAL SYSTEMS ARE CONNECTIONS OF THINGS SO HIGHLY ORDERED THAT THEY REPEAT.

Myth 14. **TREES ARE CONTINUOUSLY FORMING WOOD
FROM BUD BREAK TO DORMANCY.**

**Most trees form 90% of their current growth increment in 6 to 8 weeks
after new leaves are formed.** Some tropical trees have periodic flushes of
growth, but still they rarely are forming wood continuously all year. Trees
under stress will often form only a small amount of new springwood or
earlywood for a few weeks after the original leaf flush. This pattern is common
in oaks defoliated for several consecutive years by gypsy moth caterpillars.

Myth 15. **COMPARTMENTALIZATION AND CODIT
ARE THE SAME.**

CODIT is a model of compartmentalization. Compartmentalization is a
tree's defense process, where existing boundaries are strengthened — reaction
zone — and new boundaries are formed — barrier zone — that resist spread of
infections. The boundaries also protect the liquid transport, energy storage, and
mechanical support systems. CODIT is a model that gives dimensions to the
configuration of the infected wood surrounded by the reaction zone — walls 1,
2, and 3. And, the barrier zone is called wall 4. The CODIT model makes it easy
to indicate the shape or configuration of the infected wood. (See A for details,
and X-263, 264, 265, 302, 303, 323, 330, and 335.)

Myth 16. **THE BOUNDARIES IN COMPARTMENTALIZATION
STOP THE SPREAD OF DECAY.**

The boundaries resist, not stop, the spread of decay. The reaction zone may
be weak or strong. The invading microorganisms may be weak or strong in
aggressiveness. (For diagrams of these interactions, see page 79 in M.) The
barrier zone can be ruptured by insect borers, internal cracks, wedges formed
by canker rots, and by ram's horns that form when woundwood grows rapidly.
(In M, see pages 141 and 181.) Barrier zones that are not ruptured do limit the
radial spread of infections. That is why there are hollows in trees where the
hollow is surrounded by sound sapwood or heartwood.

Myth 17.   MOISTURE ALONE ACCOUNTS FOR THE
PATTERNS OF DECAY IN TREES.
The boundaries have been chemically characterized and their strength is under moderate to strong genetic control. Most of the boundaries contain suberin. (See X-264, 265.) The barrier zone is an anatomical and chemical boundary. The boundaries do maintain high moisture levels in the wood, and high moisture is a deterrent factor to spread of decay. Low moisture is also a deterrent to spread of decay (X-193). (For more on suberin, see Pearce, R.B., 1990, Eur. J. For. Path. 20: 275-289; and for more on moisture and decay, see Boddy, L. and A.D. Rayner, 1983, New Phytol. 94: 623-641.)

Myth 18.   PRUNE LIVING AND DEAD BRANCHES
FLUSH WITH THE TRUNK.
Flush cuts destroy the tissues that form the branch protection zone. There is much more! Flush cuts injure the trunk above and below the branch. Rapid formation of callus and woundwood to the sides of the wound often result in rams' horns that start internal cracks, and hazardous trees. The wounds deplete energy reserves, and infestations by insects, and infections by canker-causing, and decay-causing microorganisms often spread rapidly deep into the trunk. (For more see A and H, and diagrams on pages 16 and 17, and X-23, 29, 79, 91, 93, 143, 373, and 391.)

Myth 19.   THERE IS A SET ANGLE
FOR A CORRECT PRUNING CUT.
The size of the swollen collar at the branch base determines the position and angle of a correct cut. The sizes and shapes of collars may vary greatly in the same tree. On some trees, as the branches begin to die, the collars become more pronounced (H). (See diagram on page 18.)

Myth 20.   IT IS STILL BEST TO FLUSH CUT CONIFERS
BECAUSE RESIN SEALS THE WOUNDS AND FLUSH CUTS
ENSURE MORE CLEAR LUMBER.
Resin pockets block the impregnation of wood preservatives. When the resin breaks down, the fungi have easy access to the wood, thus causing rot in construction timbers and utility poles. Flush cuts also often start cracks that can ruin lumber. (See diagram on page 19.)

Myth 21.   THE BRANCH ATTACHMENT CONCEPT
          IS NOT SUPPORTED BY HISTOLOGICAL STUDIES.
   The photo is a radial longitudinal section through a branch connection in
American elm. It consists of 56 individual photographs made by Mr. Kenneth
Dudzik, U.S. Forest Service. A shows the vessels above the crotch and B shows
the vessels in the crotch. C shows the orientation of the rays. B and C have all
the anatomical characteristics of a transverse section because the tissues are
aligned at right angles to the stem because of the collar. (See my paper in Can.
J. Bot., M-186, and chapter 12 in A for much more.)

Myth 22. **THERE ARE NO SUCH THINGS**
AS BRANCH AND TRUNK COLLARS.
Branch collars and trunk collars are shown below in paper birch. The
collars are collectively called branch collars. Anyone who has split wood has
seen thousands of the collars, yet some people say they do not exist. Some
people have seen the pull-apart diagram of the collars and thought that that is the
way they are in the living tree. Not so! In the tree the collars join and overlap
as shown here. (See M 86 to 90.)

HERE ARE DIAGRAMS THAT SUMMARIZE INCORRECT AND CORRECT PRUNING CUTS.

INCORRECT

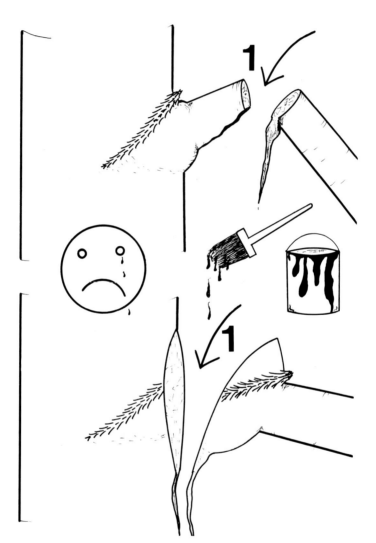

DO NOT REMOVE BRANCH COLLARS, LEAVE STUBS, OR PAINT CUTS.

Painting will not help. Wound dressings do not stop rot. Incorrect pruning starts a long list of costly problems: cankers, sun scald, frost cracks, insect borers.

NATURAL TARGET PRUNING

CORRECT

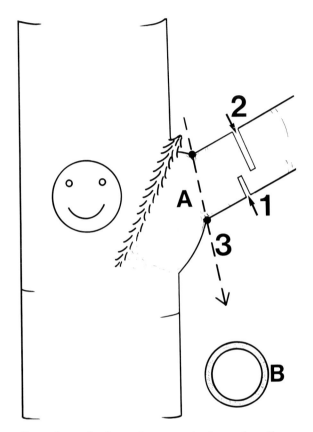

Cut where the branch meets the branch collar.

First make cuts as shown by arrows 1 and 2.
Make final cuts at 3, as close as possible to the outside of the branch collar (A).
A "doughnut" or circle of callus will form around correct cuts (B).

CAUTION

Homeowners and others who are not qualified tree care professionals should NEVER prune trees near power lines, NEVER use a chainsaw for pruning, and NEVER get on a ladder to prune. Even if you think you can do the job yourself, it is better, wiser, and safer to discuss your trees with a tree care professional first. Be sure your professional has insurance.
Do not take chances!

THERE IS NO SET ANGLE FOR A CORRECT CUT.

ALL CORRECT CUTS.

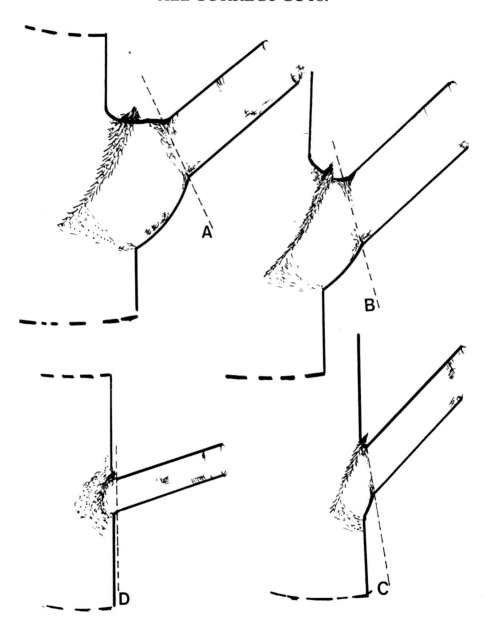

The size of the collar determines the correct position of the pruning cut.
The collar may be large (A), medium (B), or flat (C and D).

Myth FLUSH CUTS ARE BEST FOR CONIFERS.

Resin soaked the wood above and below the flush cut at left on this white pine. The correct cut is at the right of the sample. Resin-soaked wood does not accept wood preservatives. When resin breaks down, the wood is infected rapidly by decay-causing fungi. (From myth 20, page 13.)

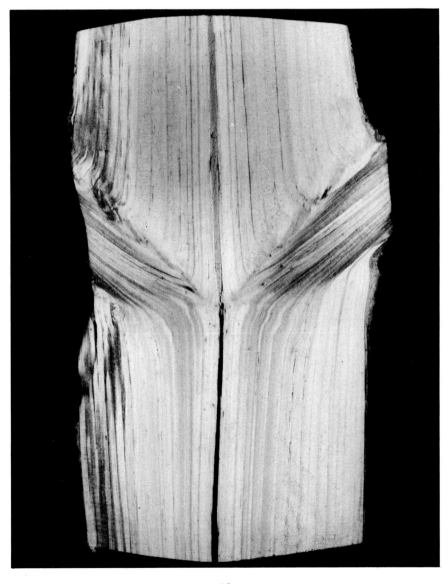

19

Myth 23.   RAPID CLOSURE OF WOUNDS
               AND PRUNING CUTS IS BENEFICIAL.
   Rapid wound closure often leads to rams' horns that start internal cracks and hazardous trees. Because of the large ribs of woundwood, when the ribs meet, corky bark meets with corky bark. When this happens the wounds seldom really close. Wetwood fluids are often seen flowing from such wounds. (See page 66 in H.) Note the crack opposite the ram's horn in the photo.

RAMS' HORNS IN MAPLE.

Myth 24.   THE LARGER THE WOUND,
            THE LARGER THE COLUMN OF DECAY.

Large shallow wounds cause little decay as shown at left in the photo. Deep wounds, and especially wounds that destroy the tissues that would normally form the branch protection zone, usually lead to large columns of decay as shown at right in the photo. This is why flush cuts are so injurious.

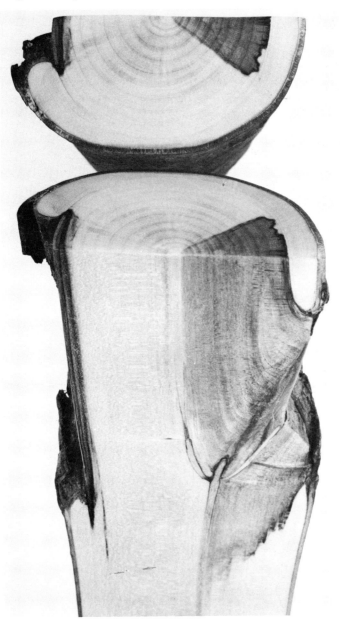

Myth 25. BIG "CALLUS" MEANS STRONG "HEALING".

Wound closure and compartmentalization are two separate processes (X-196, 323; M-93). Confusion over callus and healing were major reasons why the flush cut persisted (for a history of this, see H. Mayer-Wegelin, X-214). Actually, what was called "callus" was not callus but woundwood (see E. Küster, X-180), and what was called healing was sealing or closure (for more, see page 63 in H). The statement is a perfect example of an oxymoron. It is time to put this myth to rest!

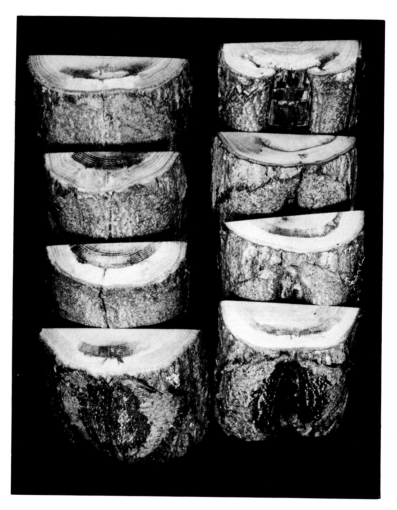

CLOSURE AND COMPARTMENTALIZATION IN RED OAKS.

All 4 treated wounds on the red oak at left closed after 16 years, while all 4 wounds on another red oak did not close after the same period. There was no significant difference between amounts of decay among all samples. For more, see photo on page 23. (See Shigo and Shortle reference M-163.)

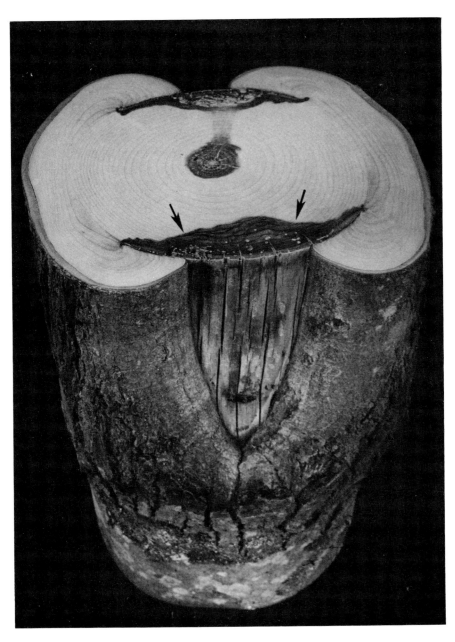

Closure and compartmentalization are two different processes. After 17 years the two wounds on the maple did not close, but very little decay spread inward (arrows). Slow closure is more the rule than the exception in nature. If decay rates were associated with closure rates, trees would not stay upright very long.

Myth 26. **DO NOT PRUNE TREES THAT "BLEED" IN SPRING.**
Sap flow is a defense mechanism. Little injury results when "bleeders" are correctly pruned in spring. If the flow of sap is considered unsightly, then the trees can be pruned after the leaves have formed. Many of the old recommendations for timing of pruning were based on timing of wounding, because the flush cut caused a trunk wound. The old recommendations really were aimed at the least or most injurious time to *wound* a tree. When pruning cuts are made correctly, the timing can be extended greatly. It is still true that small mistakes can result in serious injuries during the early stages of dormancy. This is the time when most wood-decay fungi produce spores. In spring, small mistakes can also lead to serious injuries. This is the time when many canker-causing microorganisms infect bark and wood. (For more on timing of wounding, see Dujesiefken, K., A. Peylo, and W. Liese. 1991. Forstw. Cbl. 110, 371-380.)

Myth 27. **WHEN PRUNING, BE SAFE AND LEAVE A SMALL STUB.**
Aim for the target where the branch meets the collar. If a correct cut is made, a complete ring, oval, or "doughnut" of callus and woundwood will surround the margin of the wound. The question often asked is whether it is better to leave a small stub or to cut into the collar. The answer is neither! If you cannot see the collar, aim for where you think it is. Observe trees of that same species that have dying and dead branches. Note where the living tissues circle the dying or dead branch. Some people leave a small stub because they are concerned about injuring the collar. Do not do it!

BY ASKING NATURE THE RIGHT QUESTION, YOU ALREADY HAVE HALF OF THE ANSWER.

Myth 28.   REMOVE THE LIVING WOOD AT THE BASE
OF DEAD BRANCHES.

Removal of the living wood at the base of dead branches wounds the trunk. When removing dead branches, cut as close as possible to the swollen base of living wood, but do not injure or remove it. The dead branch core is compartmentalized within the swollen base of living tissues (see photo 55 in H).

Myth 29.   CALLUS IS WOODY RIBS THAT CLOSE WOUNDS.

Callus has little or no lignin, and the cells are all homogeneous and meristematic (E. Küster, X-180). When the cells become strongly lignified, and when cells differentiate and are no longer meristematic, the wood ribs should be called woundwood (M-148). Callus usually persists for one growing season after wounding. There are gradations of changes from callus to woundwood, to wood.

Myth 30.   CALLUS FORMS ONLY TO THE SIDES OF WOUNDS.

Callus forms completely around correct pruning cuts and correctly scribed wounds. Because the flush cut was considered the correct cut for so long, the callus patterns to the sides of the flush cuts that wounded the trunk were considered normal. The tissues often died back above and below the wound. The weakened tissues above and below the flush cuts were often the starting points for cracks and cankers (A-430, 431;H).

IF YOU CANNOT DEFINE A TERM IN 25 WORDS
OR LESS YOU SHOULD NOT USE IT.

Myth 31. ANGLES OF CROTCHES INDICATE DEGREE
OF WEAKNESS OF STEMS AND BRANCHES.

Presence and amount of included bark within the crotches is more of an indicator of weakness than the angles of the crotches. Care must be taken with this subject because as the angles of crotches become more acute, the greater the chances of included bark between the stems or branches. Be very careful when selecting young trees from nurseries. Avoid trees that have included bark within the crotches. Or if the tree is already planted, cut away one of the stems or branches as soon as possible. When climbing a tree, avoid throwing a line between crotches that have included bark. (For more, see diagrams 85 and 154 in M.) If the stems that have included bark within the crotch are upright, consider cabling and bracing as a way to extend the safe period of the tree. Cabling and bracing will not strengthen the stems. Cables should always be static, or not binding or taut when leaves are on the tree.

Myth 32. BARK SLIPS IN THE SPRING.

It is the new xylem that is not yet lignified that slips. The cambial zone produces new xylem on its inner side toward the pith and new phloem on its outer side toward the outer bark. All cells in the xylem and phloem are alive when they are formed by the cambial zone. The vessels do not become functional until they die. It is correct to call the new tissues formed on the inner side of the cambial zone xylem, but not wood. The tissues become wood when they are lignified. Because the new xylem is so fragile, small wounds during the spring can lead to more serious injuries (A-179).

Myth 33. PHOTOSYNTHESIS IS MOST ACTIVE DURING BRIGHT,
HOT DAYS OVER 100F; 38C.

Photosynthesis decreases rapidly as temperatures begin to exceed 100F; 38C. For photosynthesis to occur, guard cells must be open to receive carbon dioxide. When guard cells are open, moisture leaves the plant. (See Chapter 7, X-292 and M-220.)

Myth 34. **CLEAN CAVITIES DEEP INTO SOUND WOOD.**

When treatments destroy protection boundaries, decay spreads rapidly (see photo 13 in M). Flush cuts, cavity treatments, and wound dressings were the three major treatments that set the stage for arboriculture. Sad, but these three treatments are still done by many people worldwide. Many people are saying that these old-fashioned methods must remain. (I wonder if those people would go to an old-fashioned dentist!) The popularity of these treatments is because they do not require any understanding about trees. Treatments for modern arboriculture — as with modern medicine — are based on an understanding of the patient first — tree, human body. Modern arboriculture says that cavities can be treated so long as the protection boundary is not broken (A-510).

Cleaning cavities deep into sound wood breaks protection boundaries and decay develops rapidly as shown in this treated maple.

Myth 35.   **WETWOOD STARTS WITHOUT A WOUND.**

   Many trees wound themselves as branches and trunks squeeze together, as roots squeeze together, or as woundwood curls inward about branches (photo below). Dead branches in many *Populus* species remain hard and dry at their bases. As the woundwood curls inward against the hard dead branch, the cambium of the woundwood is killed. This is a common starting point for wetwood in *Populus* species.

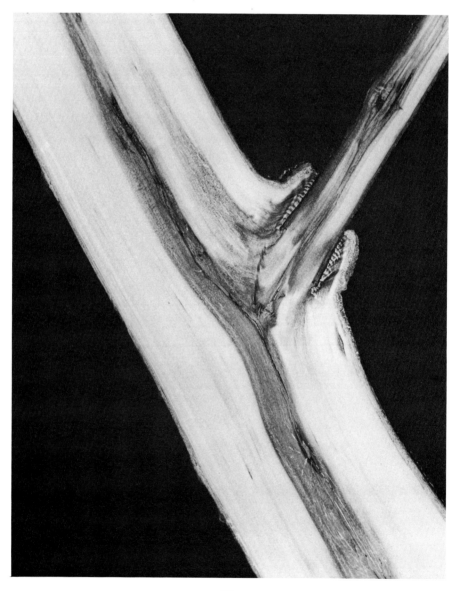

Myth 36.   SLIME FLUX FROM WETWOOD KILLS CAMBIUM.

Slim flux from wetwood does kill bark-inhabiting organisms and grass. If the fluids from wetwood killed cambium, large dead spots would be obvious below slime flux in forest trees (see photo on page 236 in A). Flush cuts to remove dead branches are major causes of dead spots below cuts. Because flush cuts injure so much cambium, the wetwood fluids may cause added dieback. Slime flux or wetwood liquids commonly flow from vertical "frost cracks" in trees. Wetwood is compartmentalized in trees (see Chapter 18 in A).

Wetwood fluids seep from an old branch stub in a black walnut. The fluids do not kill bark or the cambium.

29

Myth 37. DRAIN TUBES STOP FURTHER SPREAD OF WETWOOD, AND THE TREATMENT BENEFITS THE TREE.

When wetwood dries, decay develops (A-336, X-397). This is an example of a mixed half truth. Draining and drying the wetwood may stall the further development of wetwood in one place and enhance the development in another place. The drying wetwood often is infected by decay-causing fungi. The healthy tissues injured in the process of inserting the tube are infected rapidly by the wetwood-causing microorganisms. The tubing treatment serves to "move" the wetwood out to the bark while the more central drying wetwood is invaded by decay-causing fungi. I do not see this as a benefit to the tree.

The size of the decay column at the time it was drilled is shown by the single arrows. The double arrows show the size of the column after the hole was drilled. When drain tubes are inserted, decay spreads to the tissues about the hole and out to the wood present at the time of wounding. Note the dieback above and below the hole.

Myth 38.　THE HEARTROT CONCEPT IS CORRECT.

Heartrot is a decomposition concept that does not include the response of the living tree (see J.S. Boyce, 1948, Forest Pathology, McGraw-Hill, New York; and Hartig's famous book, X-134). Heartrot was defined as the decay of the dead heartwood. Note the rings of decay surrounded by sound heartwood in the photo below of a Douglas fir. Now we know that trees respond to wounding and other injuries by forming boundaries. Boundaries also form when heartwood is wounded. (For much more, see Chapter 17 in A, and my long review on the subject in Annual Review of Phytopathology, 1984, 22: 189-214.)

RING ROT IN DOUGLAS FIR
Old arboriculture is based on the heartrot concept.

31

Myth 39.   **WATER CAUSES ROT.**

Microorganisms cause rot. Moisture at very precise amounts is a requirement for decay. Too much or too little moisture does not support decay. The high moisture content of wood in living trees is a protection feature against the spread of decay. Because wetwood has such a high moisture content, it acts as a protection feature against the spread of decay (X-397).

Myth 40.   **DECAY IS NOT A DISEASE.**

Decay is the most common tree disease worldwide. Decay was thought to be the breakdown of dead heartwood. And, the decomposition of a dead substance could not be considered a disease (see Forest Pathology by J.S. Boyce, 1948, McGraw-Hill, New York). Merrill, W. and A.L. Shigo (Phytopathology 69, 1158-1161) pointed out that disease is any injurious process that affects the entire organism, and decay is a disease of trees.

Myth 41.   **ALL TREES HAVE HEARTWOOD.**

Many trees have colored cores that are not heartwood. Heartwood is wood altered to a higher state of protection than living sapwood as a result of a genetically controlled aging process. The age-altered wood has no living cells and is usually impregnated with substances called extractives. Heartwood is one type of protection wood. There are other types. Discolored wood, wetwood, and false heartwood are also types of protection wood that are usually darker than the healthy sapwood of the living tree (B-35). Protection wood is wood altered to a state of protection higher than healthy sapwood. Because sapwood has living cells, it maintains a dynamic defense system while protection woods do not contain living cells and they resist decay because of their altered state to higher protection. (See summary of tree defense in M, page 384 to 389, for more on protection woods.)

BUILDING A WALL IS A DEFENSE ACTION. ONCE BUILT, THE WALL IS A PROTECTION FEATURE.

Myth 42.   CENTERS OF TREES ARE THE WEAKEST PARTS
AND ALWAYS ROT FIRST.

Centers of trees are often sound while rot develops in other places. The most economically damaging rot in the world is caused by *Fomes pini* and its closely related forms (see Chapter 26 in A and photo on page 31). The rots are typical ring rots that form bands of rot within the heartwood. The heartrot concept implies that heartwood-rotting fungi grow at will in dead heartwood. And, further, because the center heartwood is the oldest, and weakest, that is the reason why there are so many hollows in trees. The ring rots alone make the heartrot concept very difficult to understand because the rots develop with sound heartwood on both sides of the columns. Ringrots follow the pattern of protection wood formed by the tree as given in Chapter 26 of A.

SOUND CENTER IN A WHITE OAK.

Myth 43.   HEARTWOOD IS A NONREACTIVE TISSUE.

Heartwood discolors and forms discolored boundaries when penetrated by wounds. Heartwood does not contain living cells, yet is does react when wounded. The compartmentalizing discolored boundaries are probably the result of substances produced by microorganisms, oxygen, and of the chemistry of heartwood. Heartwood may not be at its lowest possible energy level, and residual enzymes may still be activated by wounding, oxygen, and microorganism-produced substances. Sapwood responds; heartwood reacts. (See reference 127 in M on page 410.)

Decay in the heartwood of the red oak on page 35 is compartmentalized by a boundary of discolored wood. The arrows show other CODIT walls: 2 resists inward spread, 3 resists lateral spread, and 4 is the barrier zone that separates the decayed wood from the new wood that continued to form after wounding. Decay does not spread at will in heartwood.

A boundary of discolored wood separated the decayed wood from the sound heartwood. It is also possible that the decay-causing fungi are not able to digest the heartwood until it is first invaded by the discoloring fungi. (See my review on successions, reference 45 on page 407 of M.) If this is the case, the boundary still resists the spread of the decay-causing fungi into the heartwood because the discoloring fungi are not "altruistic".

OLD ARBORICULTURE AND MODERN ARBORICULTURE

OLD ARBORICULTURE IS BASED ON THE HEARTROT CONCEPT WHERE THE TREE IS CONSIDERED AS A PASSIVE ORGANISM, AND THAT WOOD IS DEAD.

MODERN ARBORICULTURE IS BASED ON THE CONCEPT OF COMPARTMENTALIZATION WHERE THE TREE IS CONSIDERED AS AN ACTIVE, RESPONDING ORGANISM, AND THAT WOOD DOES HAVE MANY LIVING CELLS AMONG THE DEAD CELLS.

Myth 44. SMALL, DECAYED TREES ARE BEST FOR WILDLIFE.
Large, sturdy, old, healthy trees are best for wildlife. Small cavities in upright stems support wildlife best. When removing branches to reduce potential fractures, keep wildlife in mind. Small diameter vertical snags on tall trees serve as roost sites for many types of birds. Topping destroys most wildlife trees. (See chapter 5 in A.)

Myth 45.   SPOROPHORES ALWAYS INDICATE
                   LARGE POCKETS OF ROT.
It is impossible to generalize about visible sporophores and associated internal rot. Some of the largest pockets of rot may be associated with small, inconspicuous sporophores, or even sporophores that are ephemeral. The only answer is to learn by dissections, and study the most dangerous types of rot and their signs or sporophores. Pay close attention to the sporophores associated with fractures when removing a tree. One specific fungus needs mention here, *Polyporus dryadeus*. It forms flat, plate-like brown sporophores at the base of old oak trees. It is often difficult to see because of grass or vines. The fungus causes a serious root rot that greatly weakens the tree. There are many excellent books on sporophores, but my favorite is still the old book by L.O. Overholts, **The Polyporaceae of the United States, Alaska, and Canada,** University of Michigan Press, Oxford University Press, 1953. See also the excellent new book by Dr. Annarosa Bernicchia with photos and illustrations by Dr. Fabio Padovan, *Polyporaceae s.l. in Italia.* Instituto di Patologia Vegetale, Universita Bologna, Italia, 1991.

Myth 46.   ALL MICROORGANISMS ASSOCIATED
                   WITH TREES ARE SMALL.
The sporophores of some fungi can weigh over 25 pounds, 11 kg. Yes, the vegetative portions of the fungi, the hyphae, are microscopic in size as are the bacteria. However, large masses of hyphae can form large, rubber-like plates several meters long and weighing over 10 pounds, 4.4 kg. within decayed wood. Shoestring-like masses of hyphae called rhizomorphs are commonly formed by some fungi, especially the group of root fungi in the genus *Armillaria*.

Myth 47.   ALL COLORED WOOD IS HEARTWOOD
                 OR A TYPE OF HEARTWOOD.
Discolored wood and wetwood are often darker than healthy sapwood.
Types of heartwood have been given as wound heartwood, pathological heartwood, precocious heartwood, and false heartwood. Except for false heartwood,
the other types of heartwood were probably discolored wood or wetwood.
Because of all the loose terminology without clear definitions of the tissues
under study, it is impossible to evaluate some of the literature on heartwood
formation. This is an excellent example of why clear terms are needed. (For
more, see the long review on this subject by Shigo, A.L. and W.E. Hillis, 1973,
in Annual Review of Phytopathology 11: 197-222.)

Myth 48.   WOUNDS START HEARTWOOD.
Wounds start discolored wood, not heartwood. The myth is important
because I have been told that deep injections and implants *only* start more
heartwood in the tree. And, implying that because heartwood is in every tree,
a little more heartwood cannot be considered injurious to the tree. The wounds
and the materials forced into the wood often cause long columns of discolored
wood, which are columns of dead wood. Here is an example of why myths need
to be corrected. It is possible that some poorly-informed people would not
realize that they were injuring the tree. (See chapter 40   in A.)

Myth 49.   DECAY IS A PROBLEM ONLY IN OLD TREES.
Young trees in cities commonly receive many wounds that lead to decay.
Lawnmower wounds, car wounds, crushed roots, string-trimmer wounds,
wire-bracing wounds, flush cuts and many other types of wounds lead to root
and trunk decay in young trees. The thin bark on young trees makes them
especially vulnerable to such wounds (A-15).

MANY TREE TREATMENTS WERE DEVELOPED
TO PROFIT THE TREE WORKER, NOT THE TREE.

Myth 50.   **WOUND DRESSINGS STOP ROT.**

There are not data to support this statement. In the photo below, the four wounds at left from one red maple received the same treatments as the four at right from another red maple tree. It was this research that led the way to understanding that some individuals of a species resist decay much more effectively than other individuals. The ability to compartmentalize infections is under moderate to strong genetic control. The search for new wound dressings continues, and I doubt that it will ever end. Many claims are made, but they are not supported by sound data from experiments with controls and dissections after five to seven years. It is sad when so much time and money are spent on treatments that are of no value or may even injure the tree. (See chapter 41 in A, and X-35, 68, 102, 212, and 360.)

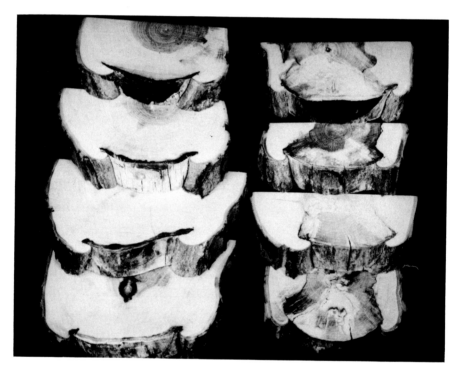

WOUNDS AND TREATMENTS ON TWO RED MAPLE TREES.

THE WOUND DRESSING IDEA:
THE REAL PROBLEM WITH WOUND DRESSINGS.

The real problem with wound dressings is not the dressing, but the idea behind the dressing. Throughout the history of tree treatments, tree mutilations were accepted mainly because some "magic medicine" would cover the wounds and prevent infections and rot. This idea gave every tree mutilator free reign over a multitude of incorrect procedures that included flush cutting, topping, tipping, digging deeply into wounds, inserting drain tubes, pointing vertical tips of wounds, and injecting deeply into trunks. The wound dressing idea has been the major problem holding back progress for better tree care procedures. Sad, but the idea is continuously being reinforced not only by people who see trees as a source of profit, but even worse, by people who are supposed to be researchers. The idea is kept alive by promises of the magic medicine coming soon. The promise has been active for at least two centuries. The idea allows anyone to become an arborist or tree expert any time he or she wishes. History shows this to be true.

MODERN ARBORICULTURE STARTED WHEN SOME TREE TOUCHERS BEGAN TO LEAVE THE PAINT IN THE TRUCK. THEN CORRECT PRUNING STARTED. ONCE SOME FINE TREE PROFESSIONALS LEFT THE WOUND DRESSING IDEA, A NEW WORLD OF TREE CARE BEGAN TO HAPPEN. (See Putting Theory Into Practice, Kevin Finley, American Nurseryman, July 1990.)

I am optimistic about the future of tree care because I know many people have left the wound dressing idea behind. I am also a realist, and I know that some people will never leave it behind because painting wounds describes the extent of their knowledge about trees and their abilities in treating trees.

MANY TREES TOLERATE INJURIOUS TREATMENTS.
THIS DOES NOT MEAN THAT SUCH TREATMENTS
ARE GOOD FOR TREES.

Myth 51.   ELECTRIC UTILITY COMPANIES
HAVE NO CONCERNS FOR TREES.

Many Electric utilities have great concerns for trees. When fast growing, large maturing trees are planted directly under power lines, there is no possible way to prune trees to maintain their natural shape. It is time to put the blame where it belongs; on the people who planted the trees! There are many tree species and varieties that are compact and small maturing and suitable for growing under and near power lines. (See Pruning Trees Near Electric Utility Lines, Shigo and Trees, Associates, and see information developed by the Utility Arborist Association, P.O. Box 542, Reading, PA 19640.)

**DO NOT PLANT LARGE-MATURING TREES
NEAR BUILDINGS OR POWER LINES**

Myth 52.   PROFESSIONALS KNOW NOT TO PLANT
            LARGE-MATURING TREES CLOSE TO BUILDINGS.

They may know this is wrong, but it is done often. Blue spruce, paper birch, and many species of pines are used often for foundation plantings. The mature size of the tree seems to be forgotten at the time of planting. Too often the annuals are in the middle of the yard and the trees are against the house. Comment — I would like to see landscape awards given for landscapes five and more years after installation, not one and two years after.

PLANT THE RIGHT TREE IN THE RIGHT PLACE

If trees must be planted near power lines, plant only dwarf or low, compact species or varieties.

Talk to tree professionals about the many choices you have for trees that have mature shapes and sizes that will fit your planting site.

41

Myth 53.   ROOTS ARE THE
               MOST IMPORTANT PART OF A TREE.
Roots and the trunk with a crown of leaves are equally important; dynamic equilibrium. The roots — woody, nonwoody — and the crown — branches, leaves — act as a seesaw in motion. The seesaw functions only so long as it is going upward and downward. So it is with roots and crown. Each is dependent on the other, and the tree system survives because there is a continuing dynamic equilibrium between roots and crown. To say one portion is more important than the other indicates a complete lack of understanding of the way the tree system functions.

Myth 54.   AFTER LARGE WOODY ROOTS ARE CUT,
            NEW ROOTS GROW AGAIN, OR REGENERATE,
               FROM THE POSITIONS OF THE CUTS.
If new roots grow, they will generate (not regenerate) from callus or meristematic points within the woody roots. Meristematic points in stems and roots are radial cores or columns of parenchyma that have a sharp point that protrudes from the wood into the bark. The spear-like points have the capacity to differentiate to form sprouts, prop roots, and flowers on stems, and on roots, the points form new woody roots. The exact nature of the trigger for differentiation is not understood, but must be tied to energy reserves and growth regulators. Callus is a meristematic tissue that can produce new roots.

Myth 55.   WOODY ROOTS AND STEMS
                  HAVE THE SAME ANATOMY.
Woody roots and stems differ in several basic ways. Roots rarely have pith and stems do. Young stems have a green chlorophyllous layer in the bark and roots do not. Stems have distinct growth increments and most roots do not. Cell walls in stems are highly lignified while cell walls in roots are moderately lignified. Vessels in stems are usually smaller and more sparse than in roots. Roots have more parenchyma that stores starch and other energy reserves than stems do.

Myth 56.   ROOTS DO NOT COMPARTMENTALIZE.
   Roots are very strong compartmentalizers. The photo below shows strong compartmentalization in a conifer root. If roots were not strong compartmentalizers, transplanting trees would be impossible.

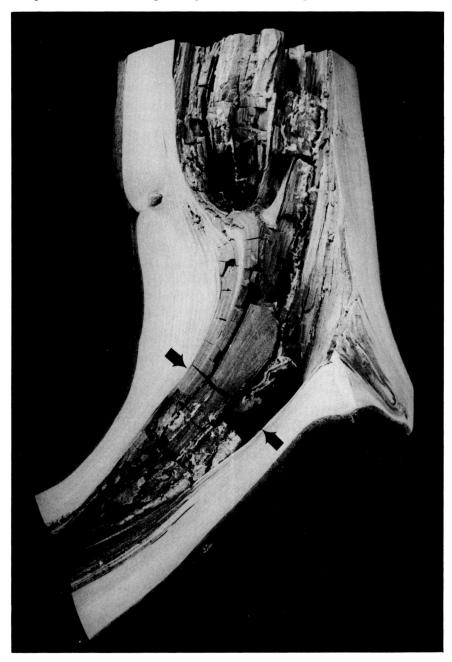

Myth 57.   ROOT HAIRS ARE EASY TO SEE
                 AND ARE ALWAYS PRESENT.

Root hairs are extensions of single epidermal cells on nonwoody roots (M-250). Small nonwoody roots, mycorrhizae, or a nonwoody root with thousands of root hairs are often called root hairs. It is doubtful that you could see a root hair with the naked eye. Root hairs are common on seedlings and on potted trees. Because so much tree research is done with seedlings and with small trees in pots, most people see the root hairs there and think that that is the same situation with mature trees. It is not! It is very difficult to find root hairs on mature trees, especially mature trees in the forest. Yes, they exist, but they are not as common as believed. The test is to take a shovel and start looking. (See front cover.)

Myth 58.   WATER MOVES PASSIVELY INTO ROOTS.

Water moves passively into roots until the casparian strip is reached, and then energy is required to move the water into the xylem (M-222). Water is transported in vessels and in tracheids as free water. Free water then loads the cell walls of fibers, vessels, tracheids, and parenchyma. The water is then in a bound state with the wall materials. This water is called bound water. When the walls can no longer take in water, then we say the wood is at its fiber saturation point. An understanding of these subjects is necessary if a person is concerned with drought and irrigation. (For much more, see X-342.)

Myth 59.   TO OPEN, BUDS REQUIRE FOOD FROM ROOTS.

Energy in the form of starch or other reserves are at the bud base the growing season before the bud sprouts (M-35). Roots provide water and elements. A tree can be cut in October or November in the north and the cut end put in a stream or pond. The next spring, the leaves, flowers, and sometimes even fruit will form on the tree. It is common practice to force twigs of flowering shrubs and trees. Roots require all the energy they can store to support their root growth.

Myth 60.   STARCH IS STORED ONLY IN ROOTS.
Starch can be stored in living parenchyma in twigs, branches, trunk, and roots. There are many patterns of starch storage in different tree species. Some trees store starch heavily in bark, others store starch mostly in axial parenchyma, while others store starch mostly in radial parenchyma. Meristems rarely store starch. The cambial zone, which is a meristem, and buds do not store starch. Starch is not soluble in water. To be utilized, the starch is converted to simple sugars that are soluble in water. Lugol's stain, or iodine in potassium iodide is used on fresh samples to stain starch particles purple. (For more information on iodine in potassium iodide, see M-277.)

Myth 61.   WHEN ROOTS ARE CRUSHED,
            OR AFTER CONSTRUCTION INJURY,
    REMOVE LIVING BRANCHES TO BALANCE ROOT LOSS.
If possible, do remove crushed or injured roots with a smooth cut with a sharp tool! When digging trees for transplanting, remove injured portions of roots with a sharp cut. Check roots on trees to be planted. Remove injured portions of roots before planting. Never plant a tree that has many crushed and torn woody roots. Also after construction injury, water if the soil begins to dry. Add a few inches of composted mulch. Watch the tree! As branches die, then remove them correctly. Fertilize with other elements and very small amounts of nitrogen after leaves have formed. If large roots have been injured, do not fertilize near the roots or you will be fertilizing the root-rotting fungi. But, if it is possible to cut away the injured portion of the large root, and if it is possible to amend the soil about the cut end, then a moderate amount of fertilizer with nitrogen could be of benefit. If sprouts form on the trunk and branches, do not remove them. The elite sprouts (M-128) may serve as a new crown (M-297, 329).

OXYMORON: COMMON SENSE
COMMON SENSE IS ANYTHING BUT COMMON!

Myth 62.   A MAJOR REASON WHY ORGANIC GARDENING
IS GOOD IS BECAUSE "CLEAN" NATURAL
ORGANIC MATERIALS ARE TAKEN IN BY THE PLANTS
RATHER THAN CHEMICALS FROM FERTILIZERS.

Organic gardening is a good practice because organic materials alter soil structure and also provide energy sources for many soil-borne organisms. However, the organic materials are not taken in directly by the plants. Except for urea (see M-235) and urea-based substances, roots rarely absorb organic molecules. Strongly charged ions are absorbed fastest by roots. In nature most of the nitrogen is absorbed as nitrate anion. (For more on fertilizers, ions, and root absorption, see M-233 to 245, and 221 to 227.)

Myth 63.   THE CAMBIUM IS A SINGLE LAYER OF CELLS.

The cambium is a multiple layer of cells (X-348). The cambial zone is thinner during dormancy than during the active growth period. The cambial zone is often called the vascular cambium. As trees mature, a bark cambium, or phellogen forms when the phloem rays join (M-54). The phellogen produces phellem, or outer corky bark, on its outside, and a thin layer of phelloderm on its inner side. The three tissues are called the periderm. The vascular cambium produces phloem on its outer side and xylem on its inner side.

Myth 64.   FERTILIZERS STIMULATE ROOT GROWTH.

This is a half truth. Fertilizers, especially nitrogen, do stimulate growth of nonwoody roots and short woody roots, but not long woody roots. Fertilizers stimulate the growth of superficial roots. The same situation occurs where roots are growing in "rich soils." Treatments that reduce growth of long roots can lead to hazardous trees because of weak mechanical support. For much more on this subject of roots that discusses a great amount of literature from many countries, see Lyr, H. and G. Hoffman, 1967, Inter. Rev. For. Research 2: 181-234. (This review should be read by all people interested in roots.)

Myth 65.   THE PITH IS A CONTINUOUS TISSUE
THROUGHOUT THE TREE.

Pith protection zones separate branch pith from trunk pith, and in many trees, the zones separate pith from one growing season to the next. Why is this so important? Because many people still believe that once organisms invade the pith, they can grow at will through the tree. Old literature cites this method of root infections that lead to crown problems. Other researchers believed that some pathogens stayed dormant in the pith for long periods and then would "suddenly" grow outward to infect other tissues. Trees survive because they have many natural boundaries that resist spread of infections. When injuries and infections occur, the boundaries are chemically strengthened — reaction zone — and a new boundary is formed — barrier zone. The pith protection zones, arrows below, are natural boundaries. When pith is infected the pith protection zones are chemically strengthened.

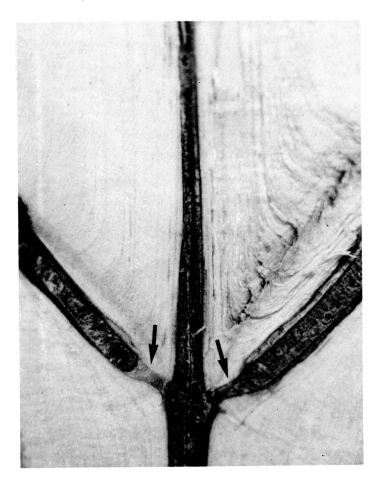

Myth 66.   FROST STARTS FROST CRACKS.
As with the sun, frost is usually the trigger that sets off an already weakened area. And, again, flush pruning has been a major starting point for frost cracks (H-45). Mechanical wounds are also starting points (see H. Butin and A.L. Shigo, ref. M-148). There are two basic types of cracks; those that start from the outside and develop inward, and those that start on the inside and develop outward. The first type are common on many orchard trees, especially apple. The cracks seldom develop into the wood. They are usually shallow in the bark. The other type starts from wounds (M-180). Rapid growth of woundwood often starts internal cracks. Then, when sudden cold does occur, the cracks split outward. The cracks are often infected by wetwood-causing organisms. In a strange way, this has survival value because so long as the cracks remain moist, the branch or trunk will sway. Also, the wetwood resists infection by rot-causing microorganisms. By understanding that frost cracks are really not started by frost now makes frost cracks preventable.

PHOTO ON PAGE 49.

The open arrows on this *Quercus alba* sample show the primary crack that formed after the woundwood ribs came together. The solid arrows show the cracks that formed as the first few ribs of woundwood curled inward at the margins of the wound. These are the type of internal cracks that could split outward after a period of sudden cold. Note the zebra-like dark stripes in the heartwood. The stripes do not follow the growth increments. The stripes are discolored wood that formed as the cracks propagated outward. The decay is compartmentalized within the wood present at the time of wounding.

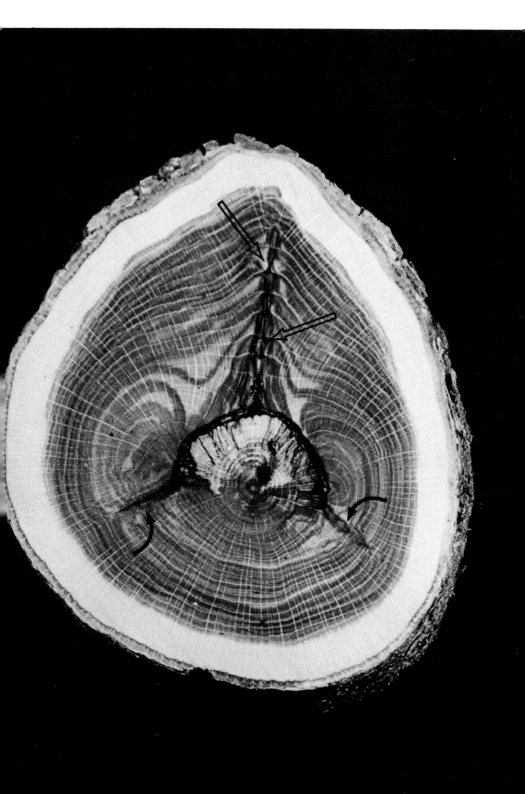

Myth 67. **WHEN BARK IS SUDDENLY EXPOSED TO THE HEAT OF THE SUN, THE BARK IS KILLED.**

Sudden exposure to the heat of the sun often kills bark or causes cracks when some wound or weakened area is exposed. The weakened area comes first. The sun is important, but it usually comes second. Flush cuts are a major cause of the weakened area. But, because the flush cut was accepted as a correct treatment, it was not considered as the possible starting factor for sun injury. The flush cut did expose bark to the sun suddenly. And, it was the exposure that received all the blame (H-121). Consider this; if sudden exposure alone was the cause, then every tree defoliated by gypsy moth caterpillars and other aggressive defoliators should have large areas of dead bark. They do not! The sun can cause a roughening of the outer bark, but seldom does the heat kill the cambium. White paints are often used to prevent sun injury. There is no doubt that the paints reflect the sun's rays. My dissections of small peach trees showed poor grafting techniques as a major cause of basal cracks. I am not certain whether there are data to support the idea that paints prevent sun injury.

Myth 68. **WIND SHAKES ARE CAUSED BY WIND.**

Wind, just as sudden heat or cold, is a trigger for circumferential separations in living tree trunks (A-152). The separations are called shakes, or ring shakes. Wounds are major starting points for shakes. The wound may start a barrier zone that separates when the trunk moves in a wind. Or, a series of small wounds, such as those made by sapsucker birds, weaken the wood, and separations develop as the trunk moves or as the wood dries (M-184). Ring shakes cause serious economic damage to timber, especially when veneer or other high quality products are wanted. In many cases there is no rot in the wood, yet the wood has no value for high quality products. (For a discussion on wind and stability of trees, see X-340.)

Myth 69.   A SHIGOMETER WILL TELL YOU
             HOW MUCH DECAY IS IN A TREE
             AND THE VITALITY OF THE TREE.
The Shigometer gives resistance in K ohms. The operator must interpret
the numbers and their meanings. The meter is a tool. And, like any tool, it is
only as good as the user. The meter has been grossly misunderstood and misused
by many people who expected the meter to give them an answer. The meter
sends a pulsed electric current and with a variety of probes or electrodes, the
resistance of the current is measured in kilohms or thousands of ohms. Once the
pattern of measurements for any substrate and its alterations are determined, the
meter can rapidly help the operator to understand the condition of other similar
substrates. The major problem that has followed the meter since its beginning
in 1970 has been the lack of understanding of trees by the operators. (See M,
pages 367-376.)

LISTEN TO THE TREE TOUCHERS,
AND BUILD BRIDGES.

I HAVE ALWAYS HAD THE HIGHEST RESPECT FOR THE PEOPLE
WHO TOUCH TREES EVERY WORKING DAY. They have taught me
much about trees. Early in my career I learned to listen to them carefully.
Loggers told me about strong boundaries in some trees. This led me to look at
compartments, and later, at compartmentalization. Many trees professionals
told me that wound dressings did not work. This led me to give up my long
search for the magic wound dressing. A little old veneer-log buyer in the hills
of Missouri told me that he would never buy a tree that was flushed pruned. This
led to the new concepts of pruning.
I believe that if more researchers would spend time with tree touchers during
their daily work, a stronger bridge could form between the two groups. And,
the bridge would not only benefit both groups, but also the trees.
Bridges must also be built between scientists and lay people. The future of
science depends greatly on building such bridges. For an excellent discussion
on the topic, see the essay on *The Advancement of Science* by Leon M. Lederman
in Science 256, May 22, 1992.

LEARN TO:
SEE, not just look,
ACT, not just wait,
LISTEN, not just hear,
TOUCH, not just watch.

Myth 70.   VESSELS ARE LONG, CONTINUOUS TUBES.

"Vessels are of finite length, their ends tapering out along other continuing vessels." (Zimmerman, H. and J. McDonough, 1978. Plant Disease, 3: 117-140). Water moves in vessels toward the leaves, and also water moves into cell walls. This movement into cell walls is called apoplastic loading. The inside of a tree is a water continuum. The vessels in angiosperms especially, and the tracheids in gymnosperms facilitate long distance transport of free water. The apoplast holds the water. When any dye is infused into the apoplastic water continuum, the dye will follow a pathway of a concentration gradient. This is why dyes cannot be used for studies on developmental anatomy.

MODERN ARBORICULTURE IN PRACTICE

Modern arboriculture means that tree treatments are based on tree biology. Know the tree and the treatments are easy. I believe that as the tree care professionals learn more about tree biology, they will be the ones that will develop the best tree treatments. Then treatments will be adjusted to best fit the specifics of species, site, and the desires of the tree owner. Also, in some cases, the practical side could come very close to the limits of tree biology. In other cases, the practical side may be far from tree biology only because of constraints on time, money, or desires of the owner. Yet, as more myths are discarded, and as tree professionals learn more about tree biology, they will find better treatments that can come closer to the best biological limits known, while keeping time and costs at a minimum. This is the direction of modern arboriculture.

ENGINEERS ARE STRAIGHT LINES.
BIOLOGISTS ARE CIRCLES.
MORE ROUND CLUSTER PLANTINGS OF
TREES ARE NEEDED IN OUR STRAIGHT CITIES!

Myth 71.   **INJECTIONS AND IMPLANTS
DO NOT INJURE TREES.**

Deep injections and implants, and shallow injections and implants repeated many times cause serious internal injuries to trees. Often it is the
material more than the wound that causes injury. High pressure also causes
injuries. The photo shows that repeated small injections into the root flare of
an American elm reduced the number of healthy growth increments to 2. Elms
normally have 12 to 18 growth increments that store energy reserves (A-526).

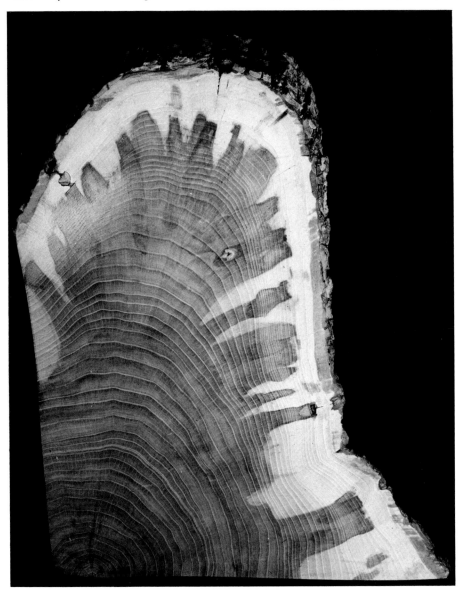

Myth 72. **REUSE THE SAME HOLE WHEN INJECTING.**
Trees wall off transport about injection holes. It is because trees compartmentalize the infected wood associated with injections that has given some people the belief that injections can be done with safety. Yes, the infections are compartmentalized, but there are limits to even compartmentalization. When injections, even shallow ones, are repeated and repeated (M-169), the compartments of infected wood begin to come together. The discolored streaks associated with the injections are streaks or columns of dead wood, not columns of heartwood as believed by some people.

Myth 73. **CHEMICALS FROM INJECTIONS AND IMPLANTS ARE TRANSPORTED IN THE SAP STREAM.**
Again, a half truth. Some are transported in the free water stream within vessels, but the chemicals also diffuse into the apoplast. It is the high concentrations of chemicals in the apoplast that cause the long internal columns of dead wood. This is typically shown in dissections by the wide bands of discolored dead wood to the sides of injection and implant holes, and discolored wood below the injection holes.

Myth 74. **PLUG HOLES WITH DOWELS, OR FILL WITH WOUND DRESSING.**
Dowels or wound dressings lead to greater internal injury. (See Hepting, G.H., E.R. Roth, and B. Sleeth, 1949, J. Forest. 47: 366-370.) When holes must be made into trees as for tapping maples, inserting rods, or extracting increment cores for dendrochronological studies, always use a very sharp drill bit (M-166). Use great care not to loosen the bark about the hole. Drill above strong prominent roots, not in depressions. If more than one hole is needed, do not drill holes in vertical alignment.

Myth 75.   TREE PATHOGENS, SUCH AS THOSE THAT CAUSE
DUTCH ELM DISEASE, OAK WILT, AND FIRE BLIGHT,
SPREAD AT WILL IN TREES.

So long as there are sufficient energy reserves to support a strong defense system, infections will be compartmentalized. The 5 pear samples below show that fire blight infections spreading downward did not spread into branches, or into the trunk portions that supported the branches. The photo on page 56 shows the same pattern with Dutch elm disease. Note the one small, clear, uninfected growth increment on the left side of the elm sample. The infection was not only compartmentalized within the tissues that were supporting the infected top, but the new tissues that formed after the infection spread downward were not infected. Why then do so many trees die? The answer is that multiple infections wall off so much of the tissues that would normally store energy reserves that compartmentalization no longer functions. As this is happening, many other dysfunctions are happening — leaf wilting, vessel plugging. Death of a tree is not due to a single, simple agent. If a major common cause could be cited it would be that the trees lose their defense system. This problem is well known now to humans!

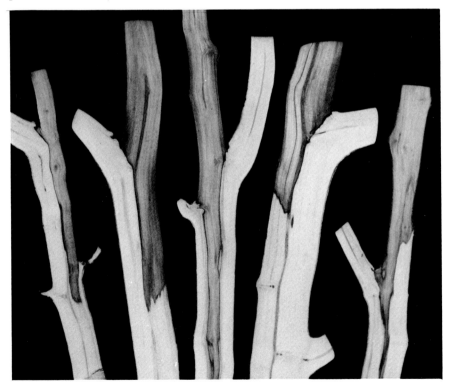

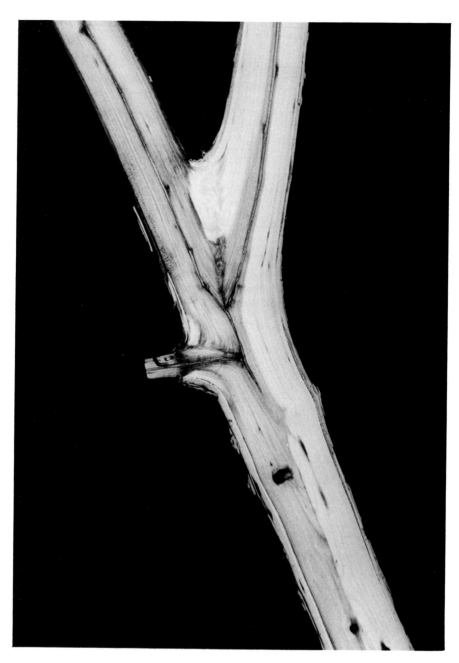

The fungus that causes Dutch elm disease spreads downward in the American elm, but the infection remained in those tissues connected with the vertical stem. The growth increment that formed after the infection remained clear in this sample because the infection did not spread into the new tissues. Infections do not spread at will in trees.

Myth 76.   IT IS IMPOSSIBLE TO SELECT TREES
                    RESISTANT TO DECAY.

It is possible to select individuals of a species that are highly resistant to the *spread* of decay. Here is a perfect example of how definitions have hampered the process of selecting tough trees. If decay is defined as the result of infection of wounds, then it is impossible to select for resistance because when a tree is wounded it will be infected. There is no way (at least now known, or known to me) that a tree once wounded can prevent infection. This is why it is correct to say injury and infection when discussing this subject. However, if decay is defined as an infection process where space — volume of wood — and time are increasing, then decay, or more exactly, but here now redundant, the *spread* of decay in trees can be a factor for selection. Since 1977 many researchers have been reporting that wound compartmentalization is under moderate to strong genetic control (X-196, 300, 302, 303, 323, and M-86, 92, 93, 97, 112, 123, 124, 155, 165). The 2 samples below came from red maple trees of the same size and age that were wounded the same way at the same time. Eight years after wounding the trees were cut. The tree at left was a weak compartmentalizer and the tree at right was a strong one. Methods have been developed for selecting individuals of species that are strong. Drs. L. Shain and J.B. Miller recently reported in Phytopathology that strong and weak compartmentalizers of *Populus* species could be determined on the basis of their ethylene production (X-323). Dr. Frank S. Santamour Jr. has been a leader in this field and he has stated (X-300, 302, 303) that trees that graft easily are usually strong compartmentalizers. So, the tree propagators have been an unseen beneficial force in providing tough, decay resistant trees for our cities and forests. Yet, there are no nurseries that are purposefully growing tough trees for our cities. Sad!

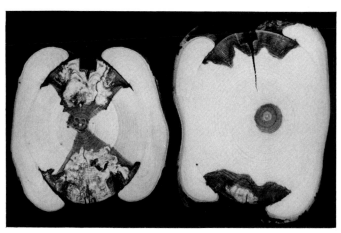

Weak — left — and strong — right — compartmentalizing individuals of red maple.

Myth 77. **MINERAL STAIN IS CAUSED BY HIGH ABSORPTION OF MINERALS FROM THE SOIL AND THE DEPOSITING OF THE MINERALS IN THE TRUNK WOOD.**

Mineral stain is a type of discolored wood associated with wounds. In sugar maple, wounds made by squirrels, sapsuckers, and especially the sugar maple borer, *Glycobius speciosus*, are the major ones. The sugar maple borer cuts a diagonal gallery into the tree. This causes a twisting of the grain as new tissues form. Many beetles do not complete their two year cycle, but still they wound the trees from minor wounds to very large wounds (See A-87). High concentrations of carbonates in the wood will often effervesce when hydrochloric acid is applied. Because the wounded areas often caused timber saws to spark, the discolored wood was called mineral stain. And, the belief was (is) that the trees "just took up the minerals and deposited them in the wood." Not so.

Myth 78. **STUMP SPROUTS WILL NEVER BECOME STRONG, HEALTHY TREES.**

Sprouts low on the stump can grow to become strong, healthy, and safe trees (A-495, M-133). If a clump of trees is wanted from a tree that does produce basal sprouts, cut the stump low to the ground. Choose sprouts from single buds. Cut away bushy sprouts. Space new stems evenly about the stump. Most sprouts grow rapidly for 4 to 5 years, then growth slows as they develop new root systems.

Myth 79. **ROT SPREADS FROM STUMP TO BASAL SPROUTS.**

As shown in the photo on page 59, rot seldom spreads from stump to sprout (A-490). When sprouts squeeze against stumps that have not decayed, a dead area on the sprout serves as an infection court for fungi. Also, as companion sprouts die away from an elite sprout, the dead stubs of the companion sprouts could act as the entrance points for decay.

58

Myth 80.   CUT STORM INJURED TREES
                              AS SOON AS POSSIBLE.
Make absolutely, absolutely, certain that the tree is not in contact with an energized electric power line! Never advise a client over the phone to begin cutting a storm injured tree. Small branches under great tension can cause serious personal injury when released by a saw cut. Cutting storm injured trees is an extremely dangerous job, and should be left only to the best-trained professionals.

Myth 81. **SCRIBE WOUNDS TO FORM A VERTICAL ELLIPSE
            WITH POINTED ENDS.**
Scribe as shallow as possible, and make all margins rounded. Do not point vertical tips. Do not enlarge the wound. Scribe as soon as possible after wounding. If callus has started to form, cut away loose bark to expose the callus, but do not injure the callus. Scribing wounds on thick-barked trees is very difficult. If a small chainsaw is used, use great care not to cut deeply into the wood.

Myth 82. **USE POINTED DIAMOND-SHAPED WASHERS
            ON THE ENDS OF RODS.**
Use oval or round washers on both sides of a rod. Seat the washer as shallow as possible in the wood (M-333, A-542).

Myth 83. **CLIMBING SPIKES DO NOT INJURE LIVING TREES.**
Puncture wounds start many tree problems (A-545). (See paper by J. Juzwik, D.W. French, and J. Jeresek, X-169.) Spike wounds were major infection courts for the pathogen that causes oak wilt. This subject is a very difficult one when it comes to pruning palms. Coconut palms have a very thick, tough outer covering. Other palms, such as royal palms, have a thin covering. Coconut palms compartmentalize the wounds very effectively, while royal palms do not. Yet, repeated injuries, even in coconut palms, can result in serious injuries.

Myth 84.   ANTS SPEED UP THE DECAY PROCESS.

Ants keep their galleries very clean and in doing so they slow the decay process (A-96). Ants live in the tree and eat elsewhere. Termites "eat" in the tree and live elsewhere. (Some tropical termites live in nests on tree branches, but they still live outside the tree.) Ants and termites follow the CODIT patterns in living trees. Termites continue to follow the patterns for long periods even after the tree is cut (A-95, M-154).

Myth 85.   ALL INSECTS AND FUNGI THAT LIVE ON, IN,
                    AND ABOUT TREES ARE HARMFUL.

It is difficult to have an exact percentage, but roughly less than 1% of the insects and fungi that live on, in, and about trees are harmful. Insects are highly beneficial for pollination. Thousands of fungus species are beneficial as symbiotes in mycorrhizae. Bacteria and actinomycetes form nodules that fix nitrogen. Decay fungi rot the base of dead branches and aid in shedding. The list goes on and on. The major point here is to make certain that we do not kill the 99% while pursuing the 1%.

Myth 86.   A HEALTHY TREE IS A TREE FREE OF INFECTIONS.

A tree can be very healthy and still have thousands of infections. The infections will be walled off or compartmentalized. Isolations for microorganisms from the compartmentalized tissues usually yield bacteria and fungi. Health means the ability to resist strain. Strain means that irreversible point beyond stress. Stress means that reversible point where a system begins to operate near the limits for which it was designed.

Myth 87.   PALMS BEING MONOCOTS
                DO NOT COMPARTMENTALIZE.
Palms are monocots and they have an anatomy greatly different from dicot trees. But when palms are wounded, chemical changes in cells about the wound do set boundaries that resist spread of infections. As with dicot trees, some palms are very strong compartmentalizers, and some are weak. Palms have a type of reaction zone, but no barrier zone because palms do not have a vascular cambium. However, there are monocots such as *Cordyline* species that do have secondary growth and a type of a barrier zone. Wounds in a dying palm lead to infections that spread very rapidly. Palms survive after wounding because of an active defense system.

Myth 88.   TROPICAL TREES ARE THE MOST MASSIVE TREES
IN THE WORLD BECAUSE THEY KEEP GROWING YEAR-ROUND.
The most massive trees are the coastal redwoods and Douglas firs along the Pacific coast of U.S.A. and Canada, and the eucalypts in Victoria and Tasmania in southern Australia. Tropical trees may be green all year, but they are not growing wood all year. Some of the prop-rooted *Ficus* species can cover a great amount of space, but for the space they cover, their mass is still less than some of the coastal redwoods. Tropical trees spend a great amount of energy maintaining strong defense systems and in producing protection wood. If they did not, they would be easy prey to an abundance of pathogens all year.

Myth 89.   TROPICAL TREES DO NOT COMPARTMENTALIZE
BECAUSE THEY DO NOT HAVE DISTINCT GROWTH RINGS.
Most tropical trees are very strong compartmentalizers. The photo on page 63 shows strong compartmentalization in a maria which is a very hard wood (A-307). The small arrows show a barrier zone. The single large arrow shows a reaction zone and the double arrows show zone lines formed by fungi.

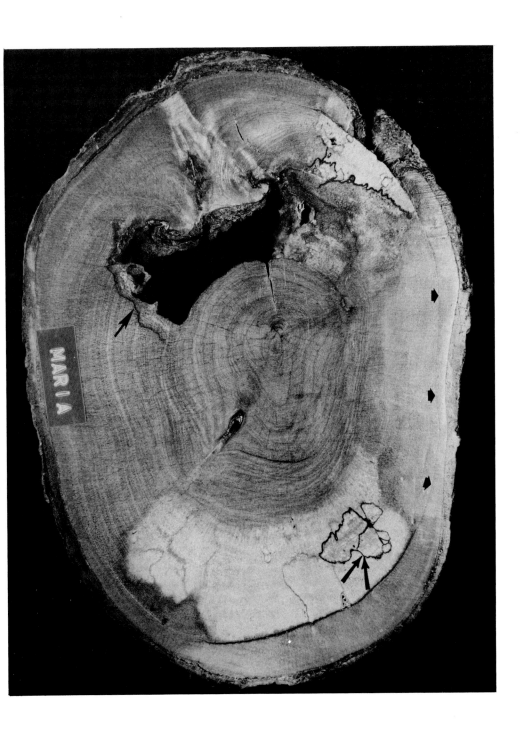

Myth 90.   THERE ARE NO GIRDLING ROOTS IN THE FOREST.
Yes, there are girdling roots in the forest but you must go into the forest to see them!

Myth 91.   ALL THE AMERICAN CHESTNUT TREES ARE GONE.
The great forests of chestnut trees are gone, but not the tree. Many trees are still growing, but most are reduced to multiple clumps where the stems are seldom over 32.5 feet (10 meters high). Some much larger trees are still alive, but their numbers are few compared to the old forest.

Myth 92.   DEAD BARK ON THE TRUNK
                  CAUSES TREE DECLINE.
The dead bark is the result, not the cause of decline. Root rots or topping are two of the major causes for dead bark on trunks. The dead bark problem is a common concern of lay people. The dead bark is very obvious to them, but not the other primary injuries.

Myth 93.   COASTAL REDWOODS, *SEQUOIA SEMPERVIRENS*,
           ARE THE TALLEST TREES EVER TO GROW ON EARTH.
Official records from Australia show swamp ash, *Eucalyptus regnans*, growing equally as tall. Unofficial records state that down swamp ash stems were measured to 400 feet (123 meters) long. In southern Tasmania, there are still some swamp ash that are well over 300 feet (92.3 meters) tall (See H-4).

Myth 94.   DRY ROT DEVELOPS IN DRY WOOD.
So called dry rot spreads only when moisture is present. Here is how dry rots develop. The fungus infects a moist portion of wood. The fungus grows into the wood to the extent that the available moisture supports growth. Then the fungus ceases to grow. But, the new volume of wood inhabited by the fungus has been altered in a way that makes it a much better reservoir for water. When it rains again, the new larger volume of wood absorbs water. The fungus then spreads farther into the wood until it again depletes the water reserves. This pattern continues as the water reservoir continues to increase in volume. There may be long periods between the wetting of the wood, and because of this it appears that the fungus is spreading in dry wood. This method of continuing to alter the substrate to favor future growth is one of the many marvels of nature (A-327).

Myth 95.   ALL WOOD-PRODUCTS PROBLEMS
                START AFTER THE TREE IS CUT.
Most wood-product problems start in the living tree. (See chapter 48 in A.) The problem here is that most studies on wood-products problems have started with the products, and not with the living trees. The patterns of decay in products usually follow the patterns set in the living tree. But, if the living tree patterns are not understood first, then the products problems cannot be related to the tree. For example, wood altered only slightly in the living tree will be the wood first to absorb moisture in a product. An excellent paper on this subject is by Shortle, W.C. 1982. Wood Science 15: 29-32.

Myth 96.   WOOD PRESERVATIVES
ARE GOOD WOUND DRESSINGS BECAUSE THEY STOP ROT.
Wood preservatives are phytotoxic — kill living cells. Copper-based substances are especially harmful. (See, Dujesiefken, D. 1992, Gesunde Pflanzen, 44, Heft 9: 303-306.)

Myth 97.   IN CLEANING CAVITIES,
                      YOU CAN STERILIZE WOOD AND
            KEEP IT STERILE BY APPLYING WOUND DRESSINGS.
This old myth will die hard. It is still with us, believe it or not! Yes, the
surface of wood could be sterilized for a short time. But, to keep it sterile is
another matter. Minute cracks in the dressing make perfect infection courts
(See M-13).

Myth 98.   REMOVE CONKS TO STOP DECAY.
Difficult to believe, but this one is believed by many people. The conk, or
perennial sporophore, is a fruit body of the fungus associated with the rot. To
remove the conk will not slow the speed of the fungus. It is also difficult to
believe that conk removal will so lower the inoculum load, that fewer new
infections will take place.

Myth 99. POLLARDING AND TOPPING ARE THE SAME.
Pollarding is a sound pruning practice. Topping is a crime against nature.
Words, words, words, again. If you asked to have your trees pollarded and they
were topped, the significance of correct definitions would become clear imme-
diately. Pollarding starts by determining the framework of your *young* tree
(M-328) and then carefully pruning back to that framework *every* year.

Myth 100.   TOPPING DOES NOT INJURE TREES.
Topping not only injures wood in the crown, but roots are injured. And,
topping leads to hazardous trees. Topping is a money wasting treatment illegal
in some counties in some states because once started, it must be continued. Some
species of trees can survive the treatment — London plane, lindens, silver maple
— while others quickly decline — birch, cherries, beech. Topping destroys a
tree's dignity.

SURVIVAL DEPENDS ON A
CONTINUOUSLY ACTIVE FEEDBACK PROCESS AND
THE ABILITY TO MAKE ADJUSTMENTS RAPIDLY.

MAJOR MYTHS SUMMARY

Many of the myths given here about trees and their treatments can be traced to a few major myths. I believe that the two major myths are that wood is dead and that decay is not a disease. Because the aim of old arboriculture is to treat trees in ways that prevent rot, and because rot is not a disease, it is not necessary to understand the tree as a living, responding organism. And, further, because wood is dead, and wounds in dead wood lead to rot, and rot in dead lumber can be treated by various materials, then why not the same treatments for dead wood in trees? Then came the wound dressing idea and along with this idea came the idea that rapid closure would stop rot. Flush cuts became the rule because large ribs of tissues called callus formed to the sides of the wounds. Because the ribs seldom closed wounds, wood-inhabiting microorganisms had perfect sites behind the wounds for growth. Liquids flowed from the "closed" wounds. And, to treat this, tubes were inserted. The myths kept building and building. One incorrect treatment was made worse by another incorrect treatment. The ideas of the major myths kept the incorrect treatments in practice. Many people still believe that there is no need to understand tree biology because some magic medicine will come soon to prevent rot. The driving force of the major myths are still very much alive and with us today. They are being reinforced by some textbooks, ads in magazines, and by some professors who do not touch trees.

THERE IS ONLY ONE ANSWER TO THIS PROBLEM — TREE BIOLOGY. UNTIL PEOPLE WHO TREAT TREES BEGIN TO UNDERSTAND TREES, THE MYTHS, AND OLD ARBORICULTURE, WILL GO ON.

Old Arboriculture gives license to mutilate trees and to blame all other problems on factors beyond control: frost, sun, drought, root rot, cankers, and the list goes on and on!

NEAR MYTHS

The misunderstandings and half truths go on and on. Many have not reached the myth stage yet, but some are close. Some of the subjects listed here are very controversial and I agree that enough work has not been done to settle the issues. I hope that by listing them here, discussions and work will follow that will help to clarify the subjects.

Myths often arise from textbooks that are written from other textbooks where the authors have had little practical experience. The textbooks just keep fortifying some myths.

Advertisements also lead to myths. The advertisements blatantly make claims that are not supported by research data. It has become so common in the tree profession that nobody seems to take notice. You would not see such advertising in a medical journal. The quality of a journal or magazine can be measured by the advertisements it accepts.

I understand that we will not solve or clarify all of these problems tomorrow. But, it is time to recognize them as problems and not keep operating as if they are not there. Recognition of a problem is the first step towards solution. Then we must ask nature the right questions. When the right questions are asked, we will already have half of the answer.

Here are some near myths.

A.   **IF THE PUBLICATION IS OVER 10 YEARS OLD,
      ITS INFORMATION IS PROBABLY NOT WORTH MUCH.**
A great amount of the older literature contains a great amount of useful information. Being unaware of the older literature has led some people to making the same old mistakes, and for others, it has meant the attempt to rediscover the wheel.

B.   **RESEARCH ON SEEDLINGS IN POTS IS APPLICABLE
      TO MATURE TREES IN NATURE.**
Research on seedlings in pots has dominated the field of tree physiology. The seedlings and the confining pot together make the results of experiments of doubtful practical value for mature trees in "open" soils. In many ways the studies are really artifacts because the condition of the experiments rarely occur in nature. These studies "breed" myths!

C. DROUGHT IS A MAJOR NEW PROBLEM FOR URBAN TREES.

This is a major mixed myth. Parts are true and parts are not. There is no doubt that any plant that does not not receive sufficient water to maintain living processes will die. This is true even for a cactus. Water is essential for life; this is a perfect truism. So, where is the myth or problem? The major problem in urban forests is that trees that normally grow in wet sites are planted in dry sites. Simple. But, there is more. Because grass and gardens are a major part of plantings in urban areas, the grass and gardens are usually watered and fertilized regularly. This may be beneficial for trees in soils near the grass and gardens. But, watering and fertilizing lead to shallow rooting of trees. There is still no problem for the trees until watering begins to decrease. This situation can be made much worse in areas where winter temperatures could drop rapidly in short periods, or in warm areas where summer temperatures could increase greatly in short periods, because roots are so shallow they could freeze or dry out quickly. My point is that drought is only one part of a complex picture that has come to urban forests because little concern is given to the trees that are being planted, to the site where they are being planted, and to the care, or lack of care, being continued after planting. Indeed, any fool can plant a tree. But, to plant the right tree in the right place the right way is a "consummation devoutly to be wished." Too much to ask for! Again, drought is real, but it is a people problem as much as an environmental problem. The answers are simple — plant the right tree in the right place — but getting people to do it bordered on the impossible.

D. STERILIZE TOOLS BETWEEN CUTS TO PREVENT TRANSMISSION OF DISEASES.

Except for fire blight and pink bud rot of palms caused by *Gliocladium vermoeseni*, I do not believe that diseases can be transmitted by the tools normally used by professional arborists. My doubts about fire blight, a bacterial disease, are mainly with the cutting of current year growth. The same can be said for the bacterial cankers on *Prunus* species. If some sterilant must be used, use common household bleach. Do not use alcohol unless it dries thoroughly from the tool. Liquid alcohol breaks surface tension and will facilitate movement of microorganisms into wounds. This subject needs much more study.

E. ADVENTITIOUS AND DORMANT BUDS ARE DIFFERENT FROM EPICORMIC BUDS.

Adventitious and dormant buds are types of epicormic buds. There is a great confusion with these terms and with the names given to sprouts. Epicormic mean *on the stem.* It means any growth on the stem after the normal growth period has ceased. Buds that are formed, but do not sprout until after this period, are correctly called dormant buds, or sleeping buds. The point is, they were differentiated tissues at the time of active growth of the tree. After this period, callus may form about wounds. Callus is a meristematic tissue. This means that some of its cells can differentiate to form a sprout, or a flower, or a root. This condition of *de nova* formation of a differentiated tissue from meristematic cells is called adventitious. Also, in many trees, radial bands or tubes of parenchyma keep pace with the increasing girth of the tree by forming pointed masses of meristematic tissues in the bark. When the tree receives "a signal" of stress, or for other reasons we do not yet understand, the meristematic tissues in the point begin to differentiate to form a sprout, a flower, a prop root, or a woody root. These structures are correctly called adventitious because they come from meristematic tissues that differentiated. Meristematic means the ability to divide and to differentiate. This is different from a meristem. A meristem is a normal tissue formed as a result of primary growth. The vascular cambium is a meristem, but parenchyma in wood could become meristematic if exposed by a wound. Then callus forms. For a current review of this subject and of root buds, see Burrows, G.W. 1990, Aust. J.   Bot. 38: 73-78, and for other buds, see Tredici, P.D. 1992, Am. J. Bot. 79: 522-530.

The wound in this red oak stimulated the meristematic point to differentiate to form an adventitious sprout.

F. PAINT PRUNING CUTS TO PREVENT DUTCH ELM DISEASE AND OAK WILT.

There are no data to support this claim. The paper by J. Juzwik, D.W. French, and J. Jeresek is often cited to support this claim and the use of paints (X-169). The authors state, "It appears that climbing iron wounds in the trunk may provide a more favorable infection court than wounds resulting from a saw." Their experiment used ax wounds, not pruning wounds. If correct pruning cuts were made, and if the pruners took off their climbing spikes, the possibility of transmitting oak wilt and Dutch elm disease could be reduced greatly. The excellent paper by Drs. J.N. Gibbs and D.W. French (X-105) again states that "— climbing irons appear to be more important infection courts than pruning wounds." If people want to paint wounds, and reduce spread of oak wilt, they should then scribe and paint every wound made by the climbing irons! **The problem here is that papers are cited but are not read.** In another paper, the author states "— elm bark beetles attacked the bark adjacent to pruning wounds." The citation given is for a paper by J.H. Hart *et al.*, 1967, Plant Dis. Reporter 51: 476-479. When you read that paper by J.H. Hart *et al.*, you will read that it was the lower trunk not the pruning wounds that were infected! (The quotation above is from page 29 in a review paper by 9 authors edited by W.A. Sinclair and R.J. Campana, 1978, Search 8 Number 5.) My point again is that what is often cited is not really what the original authors said. This is the way myths start. Regardless, it is time to clarify the pruning and painting recommendation for oak wilt and Dutch elm disease. The pruning cuts should be made correctly, not flush cuts, as cited in work by V.R. Landwehr *et al.* (X-187). The confusion centers about painting mechanical wounds, not correct cuts. Until a study with controls is done with correct pruning cuts, I believe that painting correctly made pruning cuts will not reduce infection. However, the correct cut alone *will* reduce infection, and again, no climbing spikes! When a correct cut is made, a protection zone forms and resists spread of pathogens. And, even if pathogens do infect, they will spread only downward into the tissues connected to the branch. When a flush cut is made, the trunk is wounded and there is no branch protection zone. The pathogens can then spread upward mainly, and downward into the injured tissues.

G.　　　ELMS DIE FROM DUTCH ELM DISEASE,
AND OAKS DIE FROM OAK WILT BECAUSE THEIR VESSELS PLUG.
　　This is the same as saying that people die from a variety of diseases because
they stop breathing. With most diseases, a few major problems start the
processes that could lead to death. As the processes go on, more things go
wrong. Death is seldom the result of a simple process. Yes, vessel plugging *is*
a part of the process that leads to death of elms and oaks. My question is whether
it is a major part of the starting process. I recognize that this a very controversial
subject, yet I am concerned because the diseases have been repeatedly described
as caused by vessel plugging. Some publications give toxins a mention, but not
much. I do recognize toxins or toxin-like substances and vessel plugging as parts
of the diseases, but I also believe that rapid depletion of energy reserves also
plays a key starting role. This is especially so with American elms because they
produce mature seeds before the leaves are mature. I believe that the multiple
attacks by beetles and the multiple infections can overwhelm the tree's defense
system. Please see chapter 46 in A for my thoughts on this subject.

H.　　　FIRE IS BENEFICIAL. FIRE IS DESTRUCTIVE.
　　The answer is yes! Some forests have developed with fire as a beneficial agent.
Cones of some pines open only after a fire. Other forests have not developed
with fire, and fires in such forests can be very destructive. On the steep slopes
of the Appalachian mountains, fire is very destructive. An added destructive
feature is that the fires ignite old coal mines, and piles of low grade coal left
behind from past mining. In western forests more big wood should be left after
logging. The wood will hold water and keep soils stable. Also, the big wood
provides excellent sites at the soil line for mycorrhizae during dry periods.

I.   **FERTILIZER IS TREE FOOD.**

Fertilizers provide elements that are essential for growth. Fertilizers do not provide an energy source for trees and other plants. Again, a half truth where the wrong half has become the accepted part. Many people believe that fertilizers provide trees with an energy source. A food is any substance that provides the essentials for life; an adequate source of elements that are essential, but do not provide energy, and other types of combined elements — carbohydrates — that do provide energy. Unlike animals, trees are able to trap the energy of the sun in a molecule called glucose. This is the essential energy source of a tree. From the soil, trees obtain water and 14 elements that are essential for life. The soil elements are absorbed as ions and do not provide an energy source for the trees.

Yes, soil elements in many chemical combinations can and do provide energy for bacteria and bacteria-like organisms. My point is that *TREES* do not work that way. Correct fertilization should consider the tree and its age and condition, the soil type and pH, the elements lacking in the soil, and the desires of the tree owner. The variables are almost endless.

The entire subject of fertilizers needs a thorough "clean up." Many people do not understand the numbers given to N, P, and K on bags of "plant food!" It is far beyond the scope of this book to try to clarify the subject here. (For more, see M-232-245.)

J.   **ALL LONG DEAD STREAKS ON TRUNKS**
                ARE THE RESULT OF LIGHTNING STRIKES.

Yes, lightning can kill trees, and lightning can cause long dead streaks on the trunk. However, over 80% of what has been shown to me as lightning strikes were not caused by lightning, but by incorrect pruning cuts made in vertical alignment. Flush cuts below a topping cut often lead to a long crack.

K.   THE SUBSTANCE THAT MAKES OUTER BARK
        CORKY — SUBERIN — IS FOUND ONLY IN BARK.

Suberin is in the casparian strip in roots, and barrier zone cells and other protection boundaries, and in the walls of some types of tyloses. Suberin is the substance that lines the outer bark cells and is primarily responsible for the natural material called cork (X-28, 31). Suberin is a very long chain fatty substance that has many variations to its makeup. Mainly because of the great complexity of construction, few microorganisms have evolved enzymes to digest it. We use the substance mainly for corks. There is much more. The suberin coating of the barrier zone cells provide the zone with its strong protection feature (X-264). The suberin also "water proofs" the tissue. Suberin is found also in abscission layers for leaves and fruit. Also, some mycorrhizae "sit" in a cup-like structure that contains a pore that is closed by a suberin boundary when the mycorrhizae die. When soil conditions are not conducive for closure of the pore (M-253) microoganisms could infect the root. I believe (I do not know) that water-logged soil may be one of the conditions that stalls the formation of the protection boundary. (Idea from Dr. Joanna Tippett, Australia; see X-364.)

L.   TRUNK WRAP PREVENTS COLD AND HEAT INJURY.

There are no data to support this claim. A green photosynthetic tissue envelopes the entire trunk under the thin bark of most young trees. Wraps prevent the tissues from trapping the sun's energy. Wraps over wounds and flush cut branches make conditions perfect for infection by pathogens and infestation by insects. Wraps may be of value to protect trunks during shipment. Wire or metal wraps are of value where rodents or larger animals pose a problem. Check them often to be sure they do not girdle the trunk.

M.   GROWING ROOTS WILL PUSH AWAY
        THE WIRE IN A WIRE BASKET.

The wire can girdle roots. It is best to cut and remove as many wires as possible after the basket has been placed into the planting site. The roots may not be injured by the wire until after 10 or more years. Remove other nonbiodegradeable string and strapping.

N.   DORMANCY MEANS STOP.
Dormancy is a rest period, where normal living processes slow and changes take place that increase chances for survival through periods that would normally threaten survival. In cold climates, leaves on deciduous trees fall, and cold hardy processes begin in all trees. In hot climates, leaves tan (M-259) and vessels plug. There are no absolutes in living systems. To survive as a perennial organism, a tree must rest; it must adjust to environmental conditions that do not support life for short periods — extremes in cold or heat — or periods where pathogens could be life threatening. It is easy to understand dormancy in cold climates but it is difficult to understand dormancy in warm climates. Treatments that stimulate growth — watering, fertilizing — during a normal dormancy period of a tree in a warm climate could cause serious problems. The problems are usually root problems. Again, to survive, every system must rest and conserve energy during periods that would disrupt living processes and would "cost" too much to maintain a normal state of metabolism.

O.   ALL TREES START LIFE IN THE SOIL.
In the tropical and temperate rain forests, many trees start life on other trees, and then the roots grow downward. Many species of *Ficus* are known as stranglers because they start their growth on other trees and slowly strangle the host as the roots grow downward to the soil.

P.   SEEDING ROAD CUTS IN FORESTS WITH GRASS
                        IS A BENEFICIAL PRACTICE.
It may be beneficial for erosion control, but grass in a forest is not beneficial for trees. Grass roots will often grow deeper than absorbing roots of trees.

Q.   THERE ARE INDIGENOUS MICROORGANISMS
IN WOOD OF LIVING TREES.

A healthy tree can have thousands of compartmentalized infections. This myth is highly controversial because so many researchers, myself included, have isolated microorganisms from sound-appearing wood (X-239). Indigenous means naturally occurring, not introduced. Trees are subject to thousands of wounds, dying roots, twigs, branches, squeezed stems, and many other types of openings that are easily infected by microorganisms. And, because wood is a highly ordered arrangement of dying, dead, and living cells, the microorganisms, or their propagules, could spread for short distances within the dead cells, especially within vessels. Even the smallest chip of wood taken for an isolation is extremely large in comparison to the size of a few spores or hyphal fragments. Yet, when these propagules are suddenly placed into an agar nutrient medium, they grow extremely fast and give the impression of high populations in the wood. This myth will never be settled so long as current isolation methods are used.

R.   AFTER WOUNDING,
A DECAY FUNGUS INFECTS AND CAUSES DECAY.

This is possible, but it would be rare. Usually, many fungi and bacteria infect fresh wounds. Early infection by decay-causing fungi may stimulate the tree to respond even faster (X-332). Usually a succession of microorganisms are involved in the processes that occur after wounding (See Shigo reference 24 in M). A succession means that many microorganisms are involved. It does not mean that the same sequence occurs every time.

MASS/ENERGY RATIO

NO SYSTEM WILL SURVIVE WHEN GROWTH—MASS—BEGINS TO EXCEED ENERGY AVAILABLE TO MAINTAIN HIGH ORDER.

S. **LIMBS JUST DROP DURING HOT, DRY WEATHER.**
When heat dries wetwood in cracks, fractures often follow. Nothing just happens in nature. There must be a cause. If heat alone was the complete cause, every branch should drop. There must be another factor that is increased when long periods of dry heat occur. Old flush cuts are common starting points for internal cracks that are infected by wetwood-causing microorganisms. Internal cracks could also occur over periods of bending in high winds (A-487, B-65, H-125, and see limb drop in X-130). Decay is seldom associated with the fractures, which also leads to cracks and wetwood as a possible cause.

T. **WHEN IN DOUBT ABOUT
WHETHER A TREE IS A HAZARD OR NOT,
IT IS BETTER AND SAFER TO REMOVE IT.**
Before considering the removal of a tree, first consider the removal of the possible target (see photos 6 and 9 in M). If every tree that was considered a hazard was removed there would not be many trees in our cities. It is time to bring some common sense to this subject. Most of the trees that are a high risk for failure are very obvious. More attention should be focused on cracks. It is easy to see or measure rot, so most of the decisions are based on rot or fruit bodies of fungi. Here again, some rot patterns and some fruit bodies do indicate serious problems, while others do not. The broad brushes or generalities must be put aside for more understanding of specific cases and conditions (See M, 318-325). What is needed is a record of autopsies after failure.

U. **TRUNKS AND BRANCHES FRACTURE
ONLY WHERE EXTENSIVE ROT IS PRESENT.**
Internal cracks without rot are major starting points for fractures. This is not to say that pockets of extensive rot do not lead to fractures. My point is that cracks are often overlooked and rot is often given more emphasis than warranted. Columns of rot with cracks on opposite sides of a trunk or branch do indicate high risk for fracture (H-74).

V. **ONLY LEAVES PHOTOSYNTHESIZE.**
Chlorophyll in cortex and in other tissues in the bark of many young trees (M-287) and in some older trees, also photosynthesizes (X-270, 273). Chlorophyllous cells are often found in fissures of thick-barked trees.

W. ## THE MAJOR CAUSE OF GIRDLING ROOTS
IS LEAVING THE TREE IN THE CONTAINER TOO LONG.

Improper transplanting in the nursery from the seed flat to the liner and the liner into the field or the next container cause the most serious girdling-root problems. (Courtesy of Dr. Richard W. Harris, author of *Arboriculture.*)

X. ## PHOSPHORUS STIMULATES ROOT GROWTH.

Phosphorus is an essential element for growth of roots and other parts of plants. Because phosphorus is slow moving in soils, it was applied in the planting site near the roots, or in many cases near flower bulbs. From this practice came the myth that phosphorus stimulates root growth (Courtesy of Dr. James Feucht, author, along with Dr. D. Butler, of *Landscape Management.*)

Y. ## ROOTS ARE SHALLOW AND GROW FAR BEYOND
THE DRIP LINE OF THE TREE.

Some roots are shallow and some roots are not. In attempts to correct the diagram showing deep roots, a new problem has come as roots are shown as very shallow and growing far beyond the drip line. So, as one "correction" is attempted, a new myth is started. Yes, some roots are shallow and grow far beyond the drip line, but roots in other trees do grow deep into the soil. The problem here is the same general problem consistent with old arboriculture when a simple generality or simple recipe is wanted for a subject that has many variations. Most young trees have very deep roots in relation to the size of the young trunk. Other trees have some shallow roots and deep sinker roots. The point here is that different trees in different soil types, in different parts of the world do have different types of root systems. Modern arboriculture is based on tree biology. Know the tree and the treatments are easy. But, first a person must know the tree as a living, responding organism. There are many variations on the theme of trees. There are many variations on the theme of roots. There is a very simple way to learn about roots. Get a shovel and dig.

Z.   **EVERYBODY LOVES TREES!**

Many people dislike trees. They would like to see them all go. After all, they drop leaves on the lawn! Others see trees only as another way to make money. They will do anything to a tree for a price. Sad! In our efforts to get information out to lay people it is often overlooked that some people are not tree lovers. Hard to believe, but true.

This beautiful tree was killed by people who wanted to take home a souvenir of their wonderful time in the north woods. Many people kill trees out of ignorance.

CHANGE, FEEDBACK, ADJUSTMENTS, AND SURVIVAL

Change means movement and alterations in parts and processes of a system away from an existing state or condition. All natural systems have the capacity to change.

Feedback means the ability of the system to "recognize" the potential effects of the changes on the system.

Adjustments mean using those positive changes from the feedback process to alter the system in ways that will ensure continual survival.

Change alone does not come all good or all bad. Those systems that change in ways that make them less able to survive are rarely, if ever, seen.

If modern arboriculture is to survive, positive adjustments must be made on the basis of an active feedback process that in turn operates on the basis of accepting changes.

TREE EDUCATIONAL MATERIALS
BY
DR. ALEX L. SHIGO

ORDER
CODE

BOOKS

A. A NEW TREE BIOLOGY — hard cover, 636 pages and **DICTIONARY** soft cover, 144 pages. (Sold only as a set).
C. TREE BASICS —soft cover, 40 pages, what every person needs to know about trees.
H. TREE PRUNING — hard cover, 127 full-color photos, 192 pages.
M. MODERN ABORICULTURE — hard cover, 311 diagrams, 16 photos, 440 pages.
F. ABORICULTURA MODERNA COMPENDIO —Soft cover, 160 pages, Spanish.
R. 100 TREE MYTHS — soft cover, 80 pages, 100 myths, 26 near myths.
S. TREE ANATOMY — Hard cover, 104 pages, micro views, 94 large full-color photos.

VIDEO

Q. A CLOSER LOOK AT TREES — 2 hour video under a low power microscope.

SLIDE PACKAGES

J. TREE PRUNING slides — 125 color slides from the book,with script.
N. MODERN ABORICULTURE slides — 120 new color slides and script.
T. TREE ANATOMY, BELOW GROUND — 80 color slides, script, and audio tape.
U. TREE ANATOMY, ABOVE GROUND — 80 color slides, script, and audio tape.

BOOKLETS, BROCHURES, PAMPHLETS and POSTERS

D. NEW TREE HEALTH — 12 page full color booklet.
L. CARING FOR YOUNG TREES — 12 panel color brochure.
K. PRUNING TREES NEAR ELECTRIC UTILITY LINES — a field pocket guide.
O. 5 MINUTE TREE CARE — 8 page booklet, red and green, diagrams.
E. TREE HAZARDS — 10 panel fold-out brochure, 13 diagrams.
G. TOUCH TREES poster — A fold-out green ball is the tree crown.

For More Information, Contact:
Shigo and Trees, Associates
P. O. Box 769, Durham, NH 03824-0769

Back Cover — Gambel oak, *Quercus gambelii*, from Utah showing only a very few open vessels. The purple stain in the parenchyma indicates starch. Most of the vessels are plugged by tyloses. Trees with these features are highly resistant to drought.